Key Stage 3
Developing Numeracy

HANDLING DATA

ACTIVITIES FOR TEACHING NUMERACY

year 7

Hilary Koll and Steve Mills

A & C BLACK

Contents

Probability

Answers

Published 2004 by A & C Black Publishers Limited
37 Soho Square, London W1D 3QZ
www.acblack.com

ISBN 0-7136-6477-0

Copyright text © Hilary Koll and Steve Mills, 2004
Copyright illustrations © David Benham, 2004
Copyright cover illustration © Paul Cemmick, 2004
Editors: Lynne Williamson and Marie Lister

The extracts on page 44 are taken from *The Mirror* (top) and *The Daily Telegraph* (bottom).

The authors and publishers would like to thank David Chadwick, Corinne McCrum and Jane McNeill for their advice in producing this series of books.

A CIP catalogue record for this book is available from the British Library.

Printed in Great Britain by St Edmundsbury Press Ltd, Bury St Edmunds, Suffolk.

A & C Black uses paper produced with elemental chlorine-free pulp, harvested from managed sustainable forests.

Introduction

Key Stage 3 Developing Numeracy: Handling Data is a series of photocopiable resources for Years 7, 8 and 9, designed to be used during maths lessons. The books focus on the Handling Data strand of the Key Stage 3 National Strategy *Framework for teaching mathematics*.

Each book supports the teaching of mathematics by providing a series of activities that develop essential skills in numeracy. The activities aim to reinforce learning and develop the skills and understanding explored during whole-class teaching. Each task provides practice and consolidation of an objective contained in the framework document. On the whole the activities are designed for pupils to work on independently, either individually or in pairs, although occasionally some pupils may need support.

The activities in **Handling Data Year 7** relate to the following topics:
- specifying a problem, planning and collecting data;
- processing and representing data, using ICT as appropriate;
- interpreting and discussing results;
- probability.

How to use this book

Each double-page spread is based on a Year 7 objective. The spread has three main sections labelled A, B and C, and ends with a challenge (**Now try this!**). The work grows increasingly difficult from A through to C, and the 'Now try this!' challenge reinforces and extends pupils' learning. The activities provide the teacher with an opportunity to make informal assessments: for example, checking that pupils are developing mental strategies, have grasped the main teaching points, or whether they have any misunderstandings.

This double-page structure can be used in a variety of ways: for example, following whole-class teaching the pupils can begin to work through both sheets and will experience gradually more complex questions, or the teacher can choose the most appropriate starting points for each group in the class, with some pupils starting at A and others at B or C. This allows differentiation for mixed-ability groups. 'Now try this!' provides a greater challenge for more able pupils. It can involve 'Using and Applying' concepts and skills, and provides an opportunity for classroom discussion. Where appropriate, pupils can be asked to finish tasks for homework.

The instructions are presented clearly to enable the pupils to work independently. There are also opportunities for pupils to work in pairs and groups, to encourage discussion and co-operation. A calculator icon indicates the parts of the activities in which calculators should be used. Where there is no icon, the teacher or pupils may choose whether or not to use them. Brief notes are provided at the foot of each page to assist the pupil or classroom assistant, or parent if the sheets are used for homework. Remind the pupils to read these before beginning the activity.

In some cases, the pupils will need to record their workings on a separate piece of paper, and it is suggested that these workings are handed in with the activity sheets. The pupils will also need to record their answers to some of the 'Now try this!' challenges on another piece of paper.

Organisation

Very little equipment is needed, other than rulers, sharp pencils, protractors, calculators and squared paper. The pupils will also need graphical calculators or access to ICT equipment for some of the activities.

To help teachers select appropriate learning experiences for pupils, the activities are grouped into sections within the book to match the objectives in the Key Stage 3 National Strategy *Yearly teaching programmes*. However, the activities do not have to be used in the order given. The sheets are intended to support, rather than direct, the teacher's planning.

Some activities can be made easier or more challenging by masking or substituting some of the numbers. You may wish to re-use some pages by copying them onto card and laminating them, or by enlarging them onto A3 paper. They could also be made into OHTs for whole-class use.

Teachers' notes

Further brief notes, containing specific instructions or points to be raised during the first part of the lesson, are provided for particular sheets (see pages 6–7).

Whole-class oral and mental starters

The following activities provide some practical ideas to support the main teaching part of the lesson, and can be carried out before pupils use the activity sheets.

Specifying a problem, planning and collecting data

Brothers and sisters

Pose some questions that require the pupils to gather information about siblings. (Be sensitive to individuals' situations and include stepbrothers and stepsisters.) Discuss what information would be necessary to say whether the following statements are true or false:

- *More than half the people in our class have at least one sister.*
- *Less than one-quarter of the people in our class have two or more brothers.*
- *Less than one-third have at least one brother and one sister.*
- *About one-eighth of the people in our class have no brothers or sisters.*

Encourage the pupils to collect the information, and discuss ways of sorting or interpreting it.

Processing and representing data

What's possible?

Choose four cards from a set of 0–9 digit cards. Display them on the board, with three face up and one face down, for example:

Discuss what the **mode** of the four cards could be, for example:

- *Could the mode be 3? What would the hidden card have to be?*
- *Could the mode be 5? Explain your thinking.*
- *Could the modes be 2, 3, 6 and 7? What would the hidden card have to be?*
- *Could the modes be 2 and 3, but not 6?*
- *Could the modes be just 2, 3 and 6?*

Discuss what the **median** of the four cards could be, for example:

- *Could the median be: 2? 2.5? 3? 6? 7? What would the hidden card have to be?*
- *For each possible digit that the hidden card could show, what would the median of the four cards be?*

Discuss what the **mean** of the four cards could be, for example:

- *If the mean of the four cards is an integer (a whole number), what could the hidden card be? Is there another answer?*
- *What is the highest possible mean?*
- *What is the lowest possible mean?*
- *Is the mean 3.75 possible?*

Repeat using four or more different digit cards.

Interpreting and discussing results

A piece of pie

Cut out two large circles of card, both the same size but each a different colour. Cut along a radius of each circle. Interlock the circles so that one can be twisted round to show different sections of the pie, for example:

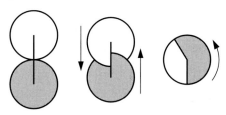

Explain that the whole pie represents a number of people. Then state what the two colours represent: for example, the red part of the pie represents the number of people who own a dog and the blue part represents the number who do not. Twist the circles to show one-quarter in one colour and three-quarters in the other. Ask: *If the pie represents 24 people, about how many people own a dog? Approximately how many people do not own a dog?* Twist the circles to show other fractions and ask similar questions, stating the total number of people represented. Then ask questions where the total number of people is not given, such as: *If the red part represents 30 people who own a dog, how many do not own a dog?* Emphasise that the pupils' answers are estimates and may not be exact.

Probability

Order, order

Invite up to ten pupils to the front of the class. Give each of them a card on which a probability is written as a fraction or decimal: for example, $\frac{1}{4}$, 0.35, 0.4, $\frac{2}{3}$, 0.85. The pupils should hold the cards in front of them, facing the rest of the class. Then ask the pupils to order themselves from highest to lowest. Combining probabilities given as fractions and decimals can create useful discussion. Probabilities given as percentages can also be included.

Teachers' notes

Specifying a problem, planning and collecting data

Pages 8 & 9

This activity explores different ways of collecting data, through conducting surveys, doing experiments or using secondary sources. Encourage the pupils to consider which people should be surveyed, or how an experiment could be conducted. They may also need

to think about the period of time over which they will collect data (such as numbers of birds). Stress that careful planning of experiments and surveys is necessary.

Pages 10 & 11

Discuss the various aspects of questionnaires, including how information is recorded and which options are given. Ensure the pupils realise that the category 'other' is often used where listing all possible options would be too extensive. In part C, encourage discussion in pairs or small groups.

Pages 12 & 13

These pages explore the differences between questionnaires (which are completed personally by each person taking part in the survey) and data collection sheets (which are completed by one person or a group on behalf of those being surveyed). The pupils are asked to list some advantages and disadvantages of both types of survey. These could include difficulty in reading handwriting, uses more resources, people can take their own time over it, takes longer, and so on. Discuss these with the whole class during the first part of the lesson. In part B the pupils can work in small groups, or you could read out the class list of names one at a time and ask each pupil to state their waking time. In question C2, encourage the pupils to use a table format to create a data bank, where information can be cross-referenced. Discuss the advantages of this format.

Pages 14 & 15

The pupils should work in mixed-sex groups of five or six; each group will require about 20 cubes and a ruler marked in centimetres. Stress that when conducting an experiment to collect data, the procedures should be established before beginning the experiment, and a clear objective is needed (this can be in the form of a question). Help to compile the results of the whole class in parts B and C.

Processing and representing data, using ICT as appropriate

For all activities which involve representing data, the pupils can be asked to use graphical calculators or ICT equipment to draw graphs and charts.

Pages 16 & 17

It will be useful to revise the mode, median and range during the first part of the lesson. The mode is the most frequently occurring item or value, and the median is the value in the middle when the numbers are arranged in order. Make sure that the pupils remember to reorder the numbers when finding the median. Discuss that different types of average are useful for different purposes: for example, staff in a clothes shop need to know the modal size or sizes, as this tells them which sizes to stock in greater quantities. The median size would not be a useful average in this case.

Pages 18 & 19

This activity explores the modal and median values of data arranged in frequency tables. Here, finding the mode is easy, although the pupils must realise that it is the most frequent value itself that is the mode, not the number showing the highest frequency (for example, in question 1 of part A, the mode is 4 not 12). Remind the pupils that there can be more than one modal value. When finding the median of information in a table, the pupils need to know how to find the middle position in a set of numbers. Demonstrate this using an example: if there are 13 values, the middle position is 7th. Show that there are six numbers in the list, then the middle number, and then six more numbers.

Pages 20 & 21

Revise the mean during the first part of the lesson, using small values that can be added mentally. Demonstrate how to find the sum and then divide by the number of values in the list. In part C, the pupils explore the mean value of a set of data arranged in a frequency table.

Pages 22 & 23

In part B, the pupils can work in small groups, or you could read out the class list of names one at a time and ask each pupil to state the number. For the 'Now try this!' challenge, the pupils could refer to a class name list.

£34, £14, £26, £28, £21, £16, £12, £22, £17, £19, £28, £24, £11, £16, £23, £25, £15, £30, £20, £21

Pages 24 & 25

The data collection in part C could be extended to include a class project, where the pupils find the most common vowel used in everyday writing in English. Emphasise that the more information the pupils gather,

the more accurate the picture will be. Small amounts of data can be unreliable. Further activities could involve looking at different languages to see whether the use of vowels matches that of the English language.

Pages 28 & 29

The pupils will require graphical calculators or access to data handling computer software to enable them to represent the data as pie charts.

Interpreting and discussing results

Pages 32 & 33

In this activity, the pupils use their own ideas to suggest reasons for changes in population numbers for puffins breeding on a Welsh island. The 'Now try this!' challenge requires them to predict further results based on certain criteria. Discuss the results in groups and as a whole class.

Pages 34 & 35

In part B, the pupils will require graphical calculators or access to data handling computer software to enable them to represent the data as a pie chart. In part C, they construct a pie chart on paper. Here, one thousand boxes of chocolates will be represented by one degree. Protractors will be needed.

Pages 36 & 37

Discuss that pie charts are useful for displaying proportions. In the example in part A, it is impossible to say the number of days being represented, because only the proportions of days in the month are shown. Similarly, in part C, the number of flights to each destination cannot be compared because the total number of flights is not given.

Pages 42 & 43

Revise how to find the different averages (mean, median and mode) from lists of values. Encourage the pupils to discuss the implications of different modes, means and medians for real sets of data.

Pages 44 & 45

For part C, the pupils will need pages from different newspapers. Include both tabloids and broadsheets and explain the difference between the two types. Emphasise that the more information the pupils gather, the more accurate the picture will be. Small amounts of data can be unreliable.

Pages 46 & 47

For part C, the pupils will need football results which give the times when goals were scored (from a Sunday newspaper or the Internet). The results should be from different league divisions. The pupils could work in pairs or groups for this activity. Emphasise the importance of writing a clear report.

Probability

Pages 50 & 51

Discuss equally likely outcomes during the first part of the lesson. Also show the pupils how to record probabilities as fractions, with the number of equally likely outcomes as the denominator.

Pages 52 & 53

Demonstrate how to mark fractions on a probability scale. Encourage the pupils to split the line into the number of equal parts shown by the denominator (for example, if the fraction is $\frac{1}{8}$, the line should be split into eight).

Pages 54 & 55

Each pupil will require ten counters and two dice.

Pages 56 & 57

The pupils will need two coins each for part B, and two dice per pair for part C. Before beginning part B, discuss how the pupils can determine which of the two coins shows heads and which shows tails.

Pages 58 & 59

In part C, the pupils explore the link between theoretical probabilities and those based on experiments. They will require coloured pencils (red, blue and green) and white card and scissors to make the spinners. If possible, provide templates of regular pentagons and hexagons for them to draw around. For the 'Now try this!' challenge, the pupils will need access to a computer program or calculator that can generate random numbers.

Decide which data would be relevant to an enquiry

What, where, who?

A

To answer each of the questions below, you could:

conduct a survey
by asking people

do an experiment
such as measuring things

find data from books,
magazines or the Internet

 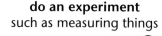  

1. Decide which is the best way to answer each question.

   (a) What hobbies are popular with 12-year-olds? _conduct a survey_

   (b) How heavy are garden birds? _____

   (c) How fast can people of different ages run? _____

   (d) What proportion of TV programmes are dramas? _____

   (e) How many cars pass your school gates each day? _____

   (f) Are more people born in July than in any other month? _____

   (g) Is EastEnders the most popular soap? _____

   (h) Do most children have at least one sister? _____

   (i) Which animal lives the longest? _____

   (j) Do tall people have big feet? _____

   (k) At what age do young people get a mobile phone? _____

2. Discuss your answers with a partner. Do you always agree?

B

Explain **where** you would conduct a survey to help you answer these questions. Decide **whom** you would ask.

(a) What hobbies are popular with 12-year-olds?
_____
_____

(b) How much do people spend when shopping at the weekend?
_____
_____

(c) How often do badminton players play?
_____
_____

(d) What are the most common illnesses of elderly people?
_____
_____

(e) What type of books do teenagers like to read?
_____
_____

(f) What flavour of milkshake do people like best?
_____
_____

 When you conduct a survey and ask people their opinions, you need to choose people who are relevant to the survey. This will give you a better answer.

**Developing Numeracy
Handling Data
Year 7**
© A & C BLACK

8

What, where, who?

C 1. Describe what **experiment** you would carry out to help you answer these questions. Give as much detail as you can.

Think about the size of the group you will investigate, and how you will measure. **!**

(a) Do tall people have large hands?

> *I would sample 20 people and measure from...*

(b) Which is the most common bird in the school grounds?

(c) Do most people in your class have hair longer than 10 cm?

(d) What is the average length of a pencil case?

2. For each situation above, say whether your experiment will give an accurate answer, or whether more data might be necessary.

(a) _____

(b) _____

(c) _____

(d) _____

NOW TRY THIS!

You could do an experiment or conduct a survey to answer this question:

> At what time do most teachers arrive at your school each day?

- Write an explanation of the advantages and disadvantages of both methods.
- Which method do you think would provide the most accurate data?

There are three main ways of collecting data:
(i)   conduct a survey by asking people questions;
(ii) do an experiment by measuring or counting;
(iii) look in books or magazines, or on the Internet (use **secondary** sources).
Methods (i) and (ii) use **primary** sources. Method (iii) uses **secondary** sources.

Questionnaire quandary

A Read these two questionnaires.

One is much better than the other.

Questionnaire
Do you watch TV?
How often do you watch it?
For how long do you watch it?
What is your favourite type of programme?
What is your favourite programme?

1. Do you watch TV? yes ☐ no ☐ (If no, stop survey now.)

2. How often do you watch TV?
   every day ☐ most days ☐ once or twice a week ☐
   less than once a week ☐ other _____

3. For about how many hours a day do you watch TV?
   less than 1 hour ☐ about 1–2 hours ☐
   about 2–4 hours ☐ more than 4 hours ☐

4. What are your favourite types of programme? (Tick as many as you like.)
   comedies ☐ soaps ☐ news ☐ documentaries ☐
   reality TV ☐ wildlife ☐ films ☐ children's ☐
   cartoons ☐ dramas ☐ other _____

5. What is your favourite programme? _____

Give reasons why the second questionnaire is better. _____
_____
_____
_____

B Mike is asked to fill in the second questionnaire.

(a) Explain why he will find it difficult.
_____
_____
_____

I only watch TV at the weekend. I watch about 12 hours on Saturday and 8 hours on Sunday. I like quiz shows, and my favourite is 'Who Wants to be Mega-rich?'

(b) On a separate sheet of paper, rewrite the questionnaire so that Mike will find it easier to fill in. Make sure that these people will find it easy to fill in, too.

I don't have a TV but when there's a good football match on, I visit my friends and watch it there.

Watching TV gives me a headache. I listen to the radio instead. I watch TV at Christmas when my grandchildren visit.

Our TV is always on. We only turn it off when we go to bed. I play computer games on TV.

To write a good questionnaire, you need to think about what information you would like to find out, and what types of answers people might give.

**Developing Numeracy
Handling Data
Year 7
© A & C BLACK**

Questionnaire quandary

A leisure centre manager wants to find out more information about the people using the facilities. Her questionnaire is not very easy to work with.

> **Questionnaire**
> What sport are you here to play?
> How often do you play it?
> For how long do you play?
> What other sports do you play here?
> How old are you?

(a) Discuss with a partner how these people might fill in the questionnaire.

> I come here to swim once a week for an hour. I'd rather not tell you my exact age. I don't play sports.

> This is my first time at the centre. I've come to play squash but my partner hasn't arrived. I'm 27.

> I come to football training for $1\frac{1}{2}$ hours every Friday. About once a month, I play badminton for an hour.

> I've just played squash for $2\frac{1}{2}$ hours, but we usually only play for 45 minutes. I'm in my forties. I come here as often as I can.

> I bring my children, aged 6 and 9, to judo lessons twice a week. I don't play any sports. I'm 40.

> I work here at the leisure centre. I'm 19 and I teach keep-fit for 5 hours each day.

(b) Write a better questionnaire that will be easier to fill in and will give clearer information.

> Plan the questionnaire on scrap paper first! **!**

NOW TRY THIS!

• Write a questionnaire that will help you to find out these things:

> **Do most people like pizzas?**
> **How often do people eat pizza?**
> **What are their favourite toppings?**
> **Do most people prefer deep pan to thin and crispy?**

 To write a good questionnaire, you need to think about what information you would like to find out, and what types of answers people might give.

Data collection

A Here are two ways to conduct a survey:

(i) give every person in the survey a questionnaire to fill in themselves

(ii) ask people the questions directly and fill in a │ data collection sheet │.

(a) List three advantages and three disadvantages of the first method.

Advantages	Disadvantages
_____	_____
_____	_____
_____	_____

(b) List three advantages and three disadvantages of the second method.

Advantages	Disadvantages
_____	_____
_____	_____
_____	_____

B **1.** The data collection sheet below could be used to help you answer this question:

At what time do most pupils get woken up on a weekday morning?

Time	Tally	Total
Before 5:59		
6:00–6:59		
7:00–7:59		
8:00–8:59		

(a) Discuss with a partner where you would put a waking time of 7:00.

(b) Fill in the table by asking a sample of pupils.

(c) For your sample, what is the answer to the question? _____

2. The people you asked could have been given a questionnaire to fill in themselves.
Do you think this would have made your job easier or harder? Explain your answer.

_____

_____

 Sometimes it is a good idea to give people their own questionnaires to fill in. In other situations it might be easier if you (or a group of you) collect data by asking people directly. When you do this, the sheet you record on is called a **data collection sheet**.

Data collection

C 1. Look at these two data collection sheets.

A

Person	Number of pets	Accommodation
1	4	bungalow
2	0	flat
3	1	caravan
4	3	house
5		

B

1. Do you have any pets?
(If no, stop survey now.)

yes	no
卌 卌 卌 |||	卌	

2. How many do you have?

1	2	3	4	5+
卌 ||	卌 ||	|||	||		

3. What type of accommodation do you live in?

house	flat	bungalow	caravan
卌 ||	|||	卌	|||

Which sheet do you think would give you the most information? Explain your answer.

_____

_____

_____

_____

2. **(a)** Think of your own headings for a data collection sheet. The headings should help you find information to answer this question:

Write your headings here.

Do people who live in the countryside have more cars per household than people who live in towns?

(b) What would be important about the sample of people in the survey?

_____

NOW TRY THIS! A magazine wants to find out about the different types of music its readers listen to. It also wants to know whether they prefer listening to tapes, CDs, radio, and so on.

- Design a questionnaire that readers could fill in on paper and post back, or could complete online on the magazine's website. (Think about readers of different ages.)

 In question C2, use a table format for your data collection sheet.

Class experiments

A **(a)** Try this experiment to help you find information to answer the question.

Do people's writing hands hold more than their non-writing hands?

☆ Work in groups of five or six.
☆ Place as many plastic cubes as you can in the palm of your hand (without interlocking them or placing them between your fingers).
☆ Grasp them and turn your hand palm downwards. If any cubes fall, leave them.
☆ After 10 seconds, count the number of cubes held in your hand.
☆ Repeat for the other hand.

ACME MONSTER HAND (VERY HAIRY)

(b) Write down all the results for the people in your group.

Name	Number of cubes held in writing hand	Number of cubes held in non-writing hand

B **1.** Now record all the results for the people in your class in this [frequency table]. (Your teacher will ask people to put their hands up.)

Write in this box the number of people in your class who held exactly 12 cubes in their writing hand.

Cubes held	5	6	7	8	9	10	11	12	13	14	15	16	17	18	19	20
Writing hand																
Non-writing hand																

2. In their writing hand, how many people in your class held:

(a) 5 to 9 cubes? _____ **(b)** 10 to 14 cubes? _____ **(c)** 15 to 20 cubes? _____

3. In their non-writing hand, how many people in your class held:

(a) 5 to 9 cubes? _____ **(b)** 10 to 14 cubes? _____ **(c)** 15 to 20 cubes? _____

4. Explain how the information in the table tells you the answer to this question:

Do people's writing hands hold more than their non-writing hands?

_____

_____

 A **frequency table** is a table where you can record how many times an event occurs.

Developing Numeracy
Handling Data
Year 7
© A & C BLACK

Class experiments

C

1. (a) Try this experiment to help you find information to answer the question.

> **Are boys' reaction times faster than girls'?**

☆ Work in groups of five or six.

☆ One person holds a ruler vertically at the very top (at the 30 cm mark).

☆ Another person places their fingers slightly apart at the bottom of the ruler (at the 0 cm mark), without touching it.

☆ Without warning, the person holding the ruler should let go.

☆ The other person should grab the ruler as quickly as possible as it falls.

☆ Read the position of their fingers to the nearest centimetre.

☆ Do this three times for each person. Then find the mean.

(b) Write down all the results for the people in your group.

Name	Number of centimetres			Mean (to the nearest cm)

2. Now record all the results for the *boys* and then the *girls* in your class in this frequency table. (Your teacher will ask people to put their hands up.)

Mean (cm)	1–5	6–10	11–15	16–20	21–25	26–30	>30
Number of boys							
Number of girls							

3. Explain how the information in the table tells you the answer to this question:

> **Are boys' reaction times faster than girls'?**

_____

_____

NOW TRY THIS!

• Conduct a similar experiment to answer this question:

> **Is your reaction time faster with your writing hand than with your non-writing hand?**

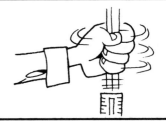

 To calculate the **mean** of a set of values, find the total of all the values and then divide by the number of values in the set. In question C1, to find the mean, add the results of each attempt and divide the total by 3 (the number of attempts).

Mode, median, range

The [mode] or [modal value] is the most common or popular value.
The [median] is the middle value when all the values are arranged in order.
The [range] is the difference between the highest and lowest values.

1. This list shows the number of people living in each house in a street.

   3, 4, 4, 5, 3, 2, 1, 2, 3, 4, 4, 4, 1

   (a) Find the **mode** by seeing which number occurs the most. _____

   (b) Arrange the numbers in order, smallest to largest. _____

   (c) Now find the **median**. _____

   (d) Find the **range** by subtracting the smallest value from the largest value. _____

2. Find the mode, median and range for each set of values.

   (a) 3, 2, 5, 1, 2, 1, 2, 3, 2, 4, 1   Mode = _____
   1, 1, 1, 2, 2, 2, 2, 3, 3, 4, 5   Median = _____   Range = _____

   (b) 1, 4, 1, 1, 2, 2, 3, 1, 2, 1, 3   Mode = _____
   _____   Median = _____   Range = _____

   (c) 4, 4, 5, 3, 2, 5, 2, 3, 4, 4, 5   Mode = _____
   _____   Median = _____   Range = _____

   (d) 5, 4, 2, 8, 4, 2, 1, 2, 3, 2, 4, 4, 3   Modal values = _____
   _____   Median = _____   Range = _____

   (e) 0, 1, 5, 0, 2, 3, 2, 0, 3, 3, 7, 5, 1, 4   Modal values = _____
   _____   Median = _____   Range = _____

If there are two values in the middle, the median is halfway between the two. If 3 and 4 are middle values, then 3.5 is the median.

A manager wants to order shoes in the most popular shoe size.
She looks at the list of shoe sizes that have sold in the last week.

Adult shoe sizes: 5, 4, 2, 5, 4, 2, 1, 5, 3, 2, 4, 4, 3, 6, 7, 7, 6, 6, 5, 5, 5, 2, 4

(a) Will she use the **mode** or the **median** to help her decide which size to order? Explain your answer.

_____

_____

(b) Which size should she order? _____

When you write the list of values in order, it helps to cross off each number as you go. Always count the number of values in the list to make sure you haven't missed any. If two (or more) values are the most popular, they should both be given as the mode.

Mode, median, range

C A magician picks some 0 to 9 digit cards. He puts them face down, then turns some of them over. Work out what the blank cards could be.

Some questions have more than one possible answer. **!**

The mode of these cards is 3

2 4 3 7 4 3 3

(a) The range of these cards is 5

4 5 3 3 ☐ 3 ☐

(b) The median of these cards is 4

7 4 4 1 ☐ 1 ☐

(c) The mode of these cards is 6

2 3 6 5 ☐ 3 ☐

(d) The range of these cards is 6

5 4 3 7 ☐ 3 ☐

(e) The median of these cards is 3

2 ☐ 1 3 ☐ 5 3

(f) The mode of these cards is 4

5 4 3 ☐ ☐ 1 1

(g) The range of these cards is 6

☐ 5 3 3 ☐ 3 ☐

(h) The median of these cards is 7

8 ☐ 3 1 9 1 ☐

(i) The mode of these cards is 6

7 8 ☐ 3 6 3 ☐

(j) The median of these cards is 4

9 4 3 2 ☐ 2 ☐

(k) The median of these cards is 8

4 9 7 9 ☐ 3

(l) The range of these cards is 5

4 ☐ 3 1 ☐ 1 4

(m) The median of these cards is 5.5

2 5 7 ☐ ☐ 3

(n) The median of these cards is 5

3 9 7 4 ☐ 1

NOW TRY THIS!

• Fill in the missing digits for each set of cards.

(a) The median of these cards is 5.5
The range is 7 and the mode is 2

2 4 ☐ 2 9 9 ☐ 8

(b) The median of these cards is 4
The range is 5 and the modes are 5 and 1

6 5 ☐ 5 1 1 ☐ 1

• Make up three more puzzles like this for a partner to solve.

Developing Numeracy
Handling Data
Year 7
© A & C BLACK
17

If there are two values in the middle, the median is halfway between the two (for example, if 3 and 4 are the middle values then 3.5 is the median, or if 4 and 8 are the middle values then 6 is the median). To find the number halfway, add the two numbers and divide by 2. If two (or more) values are the most popular, they should both be given as the mode.

Table tricks

A 1. A local council did a survey to find the number of people per household in a small village. The information was collected as a list and then presented in a frequency table.

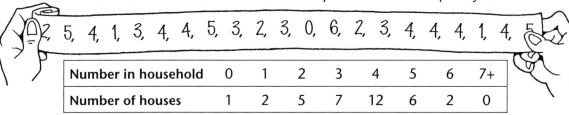

2, 5, 4, 1, 3, 4, 4, 5, 3, 2, 3, 0, 6, 2, 3, 4, 4, 4, 1, 4, 5

Number in household	0	1	2	3	4	5	6	7+
Number of houses	1	2	5	7	12	6	2	0

From the table, find the **mode**, i.e. the most common number of people per household. _____

2. The data below is for four other villages. Find the **modal number** of people per household.

(a)

Number in household	0	1	2	3	4	5	6	7+
Number of houses	1	4	6	7	8	9	4	0

Mode = _____

(b)

Number in household	0	1	2	3	4	5	6	7+
Number of houses	0	7	10	9	6	0	0	0

Mode = _____

(c)

Number in household	0	1	2	3	4	5	6	7+
Number of houses	1	0	5	17	19	1	0	0

Mode = _____

(d)

Number in household	0	1	2	3	4	5	6	7+
Number of houses	0	3	5	8	8	3	2	1

Modal values = _____

B To find the **median** of data in a table, work out what the middle position would be if all the values were written as a list.

If there were 9 numbers in the list...	If there were 21 numbers in the list...
4 numbers — 1 middle number — 4 numbers	10 numbers — 1 middle number — 10 numbers
...the 5th position would be in the middle.	...the 11th position would be in the middle.

1. Which **position** will be in the middle if there are:

(a) 11 numbers? _____   **(b)** 15 numbers? _____

(c) 27 numbers? _____   **(d)** 33 numbers? _____

(e) 41 numbers? _____   **(f)** 35 numbers? _____

Explain to a partner how you worked these out.

2. Tick to show which of these methods are suitable for finding the middle position of a set of numbers.

Divide the total by 2 and add $\frac{1}{2}$.	Subtract 1 from the total, divide by 2 and add 1.	Add 1 to the total and divide by 2.

Remember, the **mode** or **modal value** is the most common or popular value. If two (or more) values are the most popular, they should both be given as the mode. The **median** is the middle value when all the values are arranged in order.

**Developing Numeracy
Handling Data
Year 7**

Table tricks

1. A local council did a survey to find the number of people per household in a small village. The information is shown in this frequency table.

Number in household	0	1	2	3	4	5	6	7+
Number of houses	1	2	5	7	12	6	2	0

(a) How many houses have been surveyed in **total**? _____

(b) What would the **middle position** be if the data was written as a list? _____

(c) Which value of the 'Number in household' is at this position? _____ ← This is the **median**.

2. Find the median for each set of data below.

Village A

Number in household	0	1	2	3	4	5	6	7+
Number of houses	0	5	3	2	1	0	0	0

Total _____11_____
Middle position _____6th_____
Median _____2_____

Village B

Number in household	0	1	2	3	4	5	6	7+
Number of houses	0	1	0	2	3	3	3	1

Total _____
Middle position _____
Median _____

Village C

Number in household	0	1	2	3	4	5	6	7+
Number of houses	1	4	6	7	8	9	4	0

Total _____
Middle position _____
Median _____

Village D

Number in household	0	1	2	3	4	5	6	7+
Number of houses	1	7	10	9	6	0	0	0

Total _____
Middle position _____
Median _____

Village E

Number in household	0	1	2	3	4	5	6	7+
Number of houses	3	4	1	8	10	7	3	1

Total _____
Middle position _____
Median _____

Village F

Number in household	0	1	2	3	4	5	6	7+
Number of houses	0	8	13	7	12	7	2	0

Total _____
Middle position _____
Median _____

NOW TRY THIS!

• Find the **range** and the **mode** for each set of data above.

• Use this information to help you write a description of what each village might be like.

Example: Village A: range is 3, mode is 1.

This village is very small with no empty houses. I think the houses are small, as quite a few people live alone. There aren't many children in this village.

 To find the middle position, you can add 1 to the total and divide by 2: for example, the middle position of 47 numbers is (47 + 1) ÷ 2 which is 24, so the 24th position is the middle position. Now add together the 'Number of houses', starting from the left, until you reach this position. Read the value of the 'Number in household'. This is the **median**.

Being mean

A

This diagram shows the number of pupils in each class in a school. If all the pupils were in equal-sized classes, how many would be in each class?

34	29	31
28	32	25
27	30	34

34 + 29 + 31 + 28 + 32 + 25 + 27 + 30 + 34 = 270
There are 270 pupils in the school.
There are 9 classes, so each class would have 270 ÷ 9 = 30 pupils.

This is the **mean** number of pupils in each class.

The mean is not always a whole number!

For each school, find the **mean** number of pupils in a class.

(a)

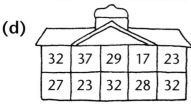

28	32	25
19	27	18
28	33	15

Mean = _____

(b)

29	35	22
20	27	28
31	26	34

Mean = _____

(c)

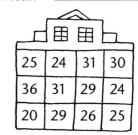

34	23	28	29
31	35	19	33

Divide by 8!

Mean = _____

(d)

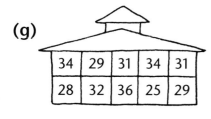

32	37	29	17	23
27	23	32	28	32

Mean = _____

(e)

36	28	31	25
24	32	30	19
37	28	29	29

Mean = _____

(f)

25	24	31	30
36	31	29	24
20	29	26	25

Mean = _____

(g)

34	29	31	34	31
28	32	36	25	29

Mean = _____

(h)

34	29	28	31
28	32	25	25
16	30	35	30
28	17	34	20

Mean = _____

(i)

35	37	31	36
29	32	25	25
18	30	31	21
25	30	34	32

Mean = _____

B

Find the mean of these numbers. Give your answers to one decimal place (1 d.p.).

(a) 3, 2, 5, 1, 2, 1, 2, 3, 2, 4, 1

Mean = _____

(b) 3, 5, 7, 2, 4, 3, 1, 6, 2

Mean = _____

(c) 2, 4, 1, 3, 2, 7, 6, 1, 5, 2

Mean = _____

(d) 3, 8, 4, 9, 2, 7, 3, 6, 5, 8, 2, 4

Mean = _____

(e) 2, 5, 8, 4, 3, 7, 7, 2, 8, 3, 9

Mean = _____

(f) 4, 2, 7, 9, 8, 1, 2, 8, 9, 4, 3, 2, 6

Mean = _____

To calculate the **mean** of a set of values, find the total of all the values and then divide by the number of values in the set.

Developing Numeracy
Handling Data
Year 7
© A & C BLACK

Being mean

Calculate the mean, including from a simple frequency table

This frequency table shows the number of pupils in each class at Meanside School.

Number of pupils per class	25	26	27	28	29	30	31	32	33	34+
Number of classes	0	2	5	9	10	12	8	2	1	0

1. How many classes have exactly:

(a) 26 pupils? _____ (b) 28 pupils? _____ (c) 31 pupils? _____ (d) 33 pupils? _____

2. (a) What is the total number of classes in the school? _____

(b) Complete this table.

Number of pupils per class	25	26	27	28	29	30	31	32	33	34+
Number of classes	0	2	5	9	10	12	8	2	1	0
Number of pupils	0	52								

2 × 26   5 × 27   9 × 28

(c) Add the numbers in the last row to find the number of pupils in the school. _____

(d) Use your answers to parts **(a)** and **(c)** to find the **mean** number of pupils in a class. Give your answer to 1 d.p. _____

3. For each school, complete the table to find the mean number of pupils in a class (to 1 d.p.).

CALLOUS HIGH

(a)

Number of pupils per class	25	26	27	28	29	30	31	32	33+	Total
Number of classes	0	1	1	6	9	11	10	11	0	
Number of pupils										

Mean =

LOW LEA ROAD

(b)

Number of pupils per class	25	26	27	28	29	30	31	32	33+	Total
Number of classes	0	2	1	4	8	10	9	14	0	
Number of pupils										

Mean =

Miserly Park

(c)

Number of pupils per class	25	26	27	28	29	30	31	32	33+	Total
Number of classes	2	1	4	3	7	15	11	12	0	
Number of pupils										

Mean =

NOW TRY THIS!

- Fill in the missing digits for each set of cards.

(a) The mean of these cards is 6.5

| 7 | 8 | | 6 | 9 | 9 | | 8 |

(b) The mean of these cards is 5.25

| 6 | 5 | | 5 | 1 | 7 | | 1 |

- Make up two more puzzles like this for a partner to solve.

To calculate the **mean** of a set of values, find the total of all the values and then divide by the number of values in the set. When data is arranged in a frequency table, use multiplication to help you find the information you need to calculate the mean.

Developing Numeracy
Handling Data
Year 7
© A & C BLACK

21

Table talk

A A mobile phone company asked 50 customers to give their main reason for buying a new mobile.

	Tally	Frequency
Buying one for first time	||	
Old mobile lost	ⅢⅠ |	
Upgrading old model	ⅢⅠ ⅢⅠ ⅢⅠ |||	
Old mobile stolen	ⅢⅠ ||	
Old mobile broken	ⅢⅠ ⅢⅠ |	
Want to change network	|	

1. The last five customers' reasons have not yet been added to the frequency table.

(a) Add them to the **tally** column.

I want a new mobile that I can play games on – my old one doesn't have them.

I accidentally dropped my old mobile and it broke!

I've never had a mobile before and thought it was about time I got one.

My old mobile is out of date – I want a better one!

My car was stolen and my old mobile was inside.

(b) Complete the **frequency** column of the table.

(c) How many people were replacing their lost or stolen mobile? _____

(d) How many of the people surveyed already had a mobile? _____

(e) How many more people were upgrading than were replacing their broken mobile? _____

2. Calculate the **percentage** of the people surveyed whose old mobile:

(a) was lost _____   (b) had been stolen _____

3. Calculate the **fraction** of the people surveyed who were:

(a) upgrading _____   (b) buying a mobile for the first time _____

B (a) How many soap operas do you watch regularly? _____

EastEnders, Hollyoaks, Home and Away...

(b) Find out how many soaps others in your class watch regularly.
On a separate piece of paper, draw a frequency table to show the results.

(c) Answer these questions.

Does more than three-quarters of the class watch soaps regularly? _____

What fraction of the class does not watch them regularly? _____

Does more than half the class watch at least two soaps regularly? _____

In part B, include zero on your frequency table to show those people who do not watch any soaps regularly.

Developing Numeracy
Handling Data
Year 7
© A & C BLACK

C

1. A group of 20 teenagers did a sponsored fun-run in aid of charity. This list shows the amount of money each of them raised.

£34, £14, £26, £28, £21, £16, £12, £22, £17, £19,
£28, £24, £11, £16, £23, £25, £15, £30, £20, £21

(a) Explain why this frequency table is not sensible for this data.

_____

_____

_____

_____

Number of pounds	Frequency
11	
12	
13	
14	
15	
16	
17	

(b) Complete this | grouped frequency table | for the information.
Group the data into | equal class intervals |.

Number of pounds	Frequency
£10–£14	
£15–	

(c) Which is the **modal class** for this set of data?

_____

(d) How many people raised between £20 and £24?

_____

(e) Answer these questions.

Did more than three-quarters
of the group raise more than £14? _____

What fraction of the group raised more than £24? _____

Did more than half the group raise at least £19? _____

What proportion of the group raised £30 or more? _____

FINISH

2. On squared paper or using a computer, draw a | bar chart | of the information in your frequency table, like this:

Discuss with a partner why the bars don't need to be touching one another.

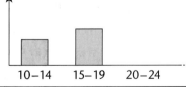

10–14   15–19   20–24

**NOW
TRY
THIS!**

• Find out the number of letters in the first name of everyone in your class (for example, 'Ahmed' has 5 letters). Draw a grouped frequency table to show the numbers of letters.

Use the groups 1–3 letters,
4–6 letters, and so on.

!

• Write a report about the information you find. Draw a bar chart of the data.

Sometimes it is helpful to group data into a **grouped frequency table**.
Make sure you use groups of equal size (these are called **equal class
intervals**). The **modal class** is the most common group. The bars on the
bar chart don't need to be touching if the amounts of money are in whole
numbers of pounds (because none of the values could be £14.50).

Developing Numeracy
Handling Data
Year 7
© A & C BLACK

Tally-ho!

A Some pupils did an experiment. They rolled a dice 20 times and counted the frequency of each number being rolled. Their results are shown as a | bar-line graph |.

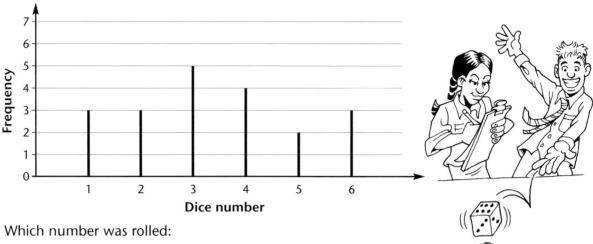

1. Which number was rolled:

   (a) most often? _____   **(b)** least often? _____

2. How many more times was the number 3 rolled than the number 6? _____

3. If the pupils did the same experiment again, would you expect an identical graph?

   Explain your answer. _____

   _____

B 1. Try the experiment yourself, but this time roll the dice **60** times.

   (a) Before you start, predict the frequency of each number.

   1 *about* _____   2 _____

   3 _____   4 _____

   5 _____   6 _____

   (b) Record your results in this frequency table.

	Tally	Frequency
1		
2		
3		
4		
5		
6		

2. Now draw a bar-line graph on squared paper or using a computer.

   (a) Compare and describe the lengths of the bar-lines. _____

   _____

   (b) Compare the shapes of the two bar-line graphs. Discuss with a partner whether your results were as you predicted.

   (c) If the dice was rolled 600 times, how many of those times would you expect the number 1 to be rolled? Explain your answer. _____

   _____

In part B, because there are 60 throws, the total length of the bar-lines will be 60. A **bar-line graph** is a useful way of showing this kind of data.

Tally-ho!

C

> **When writing in English, is one vowel used more than any other?**

1. Look carefully at this piece of text from Shakespeare's *Romeo and Juliet*.

   (a) Underline the **first 50** vowels and complete the frequency table.

   > O Romeo, Romeo, wherefore art thou Romeo?
   > Deny thy father and refuse thy name,
   > Or if thou wilt not, be but sworn my love,
   > And I'll no longer be a Capulet.
   >
   > 'Tis but thy name that is my enemy.
   > Thou art thyself, though not a Montague.

Er...cut! CUT! CUT!

	Tally	Frequency
a		
e		
i		
o		
u		

(b) Which are the **modal vowels**?

_____

(c) How many more times did the vowel **o** occur than the vowel **i**?

_____

(d) Now draw a bar-line graph on squared paper or using a computer.

   (e) Discuss your graph with a partner. Could you have predicted these results?

2. **(a)** Repeat the experiment for the **first 50** vowels of this website horoscope.

> Someone is about to take you under their wing and make you the star that you undoubtedly are. Attracting the attention of a powerful person will alter your life for the good.

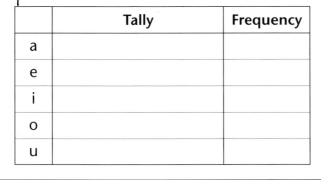

	Tally	Frequency
a		
e		
i		
o		
u		

(b) Which is the modal vowel? _____

(c) Now draw a bar-line graph on squared paper or using a computer.

(d) Compare the graph with the one you drew in question 1.

NOW TRY THIS!

- Repeat the experiment for other pieces of writing, such as from a newspaper or a book.
- How much data do you think would be needed to answer the question at the top of the page? Write a report of your findings.

Because there are 50 vowels being counted each time, the total length of the bars will be 50. A bar-line graph is a useful way of showing this kind of data. The more data you collect, the more accurate your findings will be. Remember, the **modal vowel** is the most common or popular one.

Developing Numeracy
Handling Data
Year 7
© A & C BLACK

25

Going for a swim

A This calendar shows the number of people visiting a swimming pool each day during May.

Monday	Tuesday	Wednesday	Thursday	Friday	Saturday	Sunday
			1 52	2 61	3 239	4 195
5 312	6 48	7 39	8 62	9 65	10 275	11 201
12 49	13 64	14 72	15 66	16 73	17 311	18 274
19 47	20 65	21 44	22 74	23 63	24 299	25 282
26 253	27 221	28 175	29 234	30 256	31 313	

1. How many people visited the pool on:

   (a) Tuesday 6 May? _____   **(b)** Saturday 24 May? _____

   (c) Monday 12 May? _____   **(d)** Monday 5 May? _____

2. On which date were there:

   (a) the fewest visitors? _____   **(b)** the most visitors? _____

   (c) exactly 311 visitors? _____   **(d)** exactly 47 visitors? _____

3. On which two dates were there the same number of visitors? _____

4. There was a half-term holiday during one week in May. On which Saturday do you think it began? _____

5. What do you think was unusual about Monday 5 May? _____

B 1. Now group the data into this frequency table to show the number of days in May with different numbers of visitors.

Number of visitors	Tally	Frequency
1–75		
76–150		
151–225		
226–300		
301–375		

2. Draw a bar chart of this information.

 When you group data, the groups must be of equal size (these are called **equal class intervals**). In question B1, the data is grouped into equal class intervals of 75.

Developing Numeracy
Handling Data
Year 7
© A & C BLACK

Going for a swim

C This calendar shows the number of people visiting a swimming pool each day during June.

Monday	Tuesday	Wednesday	Thursday	Friday	Saturday	Sunday
						1 195
2 67	3 55	4 47	5 64	6 66	7 275	8 228
9 54	10 64	11 64	12 66	13 72	14 261	15 231
16 57	17 32	18 39	19 72	20 42	21 197	22 242
23 49	24 63	25 72	26 65	27 44	28 353	29 217
30 72						

1. Find the total number of visitors:

    (a) in the week beginning 2nd June _____   (b) in the week beginning 9th June _____

    (c) in the week beginning 16th June _____   (d) in the week beginning 23rd June _____

    (e) during the whole of June _____

2. On which date do you think the fun-day took place? _____

3. On which date were there exactly three times as many visitors as on another date in June?

    Give both dates. _____

4. On which date were there exactly four times as many visitors as on another date in June?

    Give both dates. _____

5. Find the **mean** number of visitors on:

    (a) a Monday _____   (b) a Wednesday _____

    (c) a Saturday _____   (d) a Sunday _____

6. Find the **mean** number of visitors each day for the whole month.

    Give your answer to 1 d.p. _____

NOW TRY THIS!

● Use the information from the calendar to help you write a report for the manager of the swimming pool. Include a graph to show some of the trends. Suggest ways in which the manager could attract more people.

 To find the **mean** number of visitors on a Monday, find the total number of visitors on Mondays and divide the answer by the number of Mondays in the month.

Who ate all the pies?

A

Dr Farrell measures exactly what food he eats every day. On Day 1, he works out the **mass** of each type of food. He wants to find out the answer to this question:

On Day 1, approximately what fraction of my food was fruit or vegetables?

Day 1	Grams
Fruit	190
Vegetables	340
Meat and fish	235
Dairy products	145
Other	170

1. Key the data in the table into a spreadsheet of a data handling program and show it as a ⬚ pie chart ⬚. Use your pie chart to answer these questions.

(a) Approximately what fraction of Dr Farrell's food was dairy products? _____

(b) What food-type was about one-third of his diet? _____

(c) Approximately what fraction of the food was meat and fish? _____

(d) What food-types were about one-sixth of his diet? _____

2. Now find the answer to Dr Farrell's question. _____

B

On Day 2, Dr Farrell works out the **percentage** of each type of food he eats.

1. Key in the data and show it as a pie chart. Compare the pie charts for Day 1 and Day 2. Explain whether you think these statements are true.

Day 2	Percentage
Fruit	16%
Vegetables	17%
Meat and fish	13%
Dairy products	20%
Other	34%

(a) Dr Farrell ate about the same amount of fruit on both days.

Not sure. We don't know if he ate the same total amount of food on both days.

(b) Dr Farrell ate about the same proportion of fruit on both days.

_____

(c) He ate more dairy products on Day 2 than he did on Day 1.

_____

(d) He ate a greater proportion of dairy products on Day 2 than he did on Day 1.

_____

2. If Dr Farrell *did* eat the same total amount of food on both days, explain whether you think these statements are true.

(a) On Day 2 he ate about half the amount of vegetables that he did on Day 1.

_____

(b) The total amount of meat, fish and dairy products was about the same on both days.

_____

A **pie chart** is a circle divided into sectors so that the areas of the sectors represent the data. To estimate fractions of a pie chart, it is useful to imagine the pie split into equal sectors (for example, if you imagine it split into five equal sectors, each sector is one-fifth, or 20%, of the whole).

Developing Numeracy
Handling Data
Year 7
© A & C BLACK

Who ate all the pies?

C This data shows the mass of different food-types eaten by a chimpanzee on Day 1 of a survey.

Day 1	Kilograms
Fruit	2
Birds' eggs	0.3
Small animals	0.8
Insects	0.1
Plant matter	1.6

1. Key the data into a spreadsheet of a data handling program and show it as a **pie chart**.

Use your pie chart to answer these questions.

(a) Approximately what fraction of the food was *not* fruit or plant matter? _____

(b) What food-type was about one-sixteenth of the chimp's diet? _____

(c) What food-type was about half the mass of the plant matter? _____

Day 2	Kilograms
Fruit	2.95
Birds' eggs	0.05
Small animals	0.8
Insects	0.05
Plant matter	3.35

2. Key in this data for Day 2 and show it as a pie chart.

Use your pie chart to answer these questions.

(a) Approximately what fraction of the food eaten on Day 2 was *not* fruit or plant matter? _____

(b) What food-type was about two-fifths of the chimp's diet?

_____

(c) Approximately what fraction of the food was plant matter? _____

3. On Day 3, the chimpanzee ate half as much of each food-type as he did on Day 2.

(a) Complete this table.

(b) What would the pie chart look like?

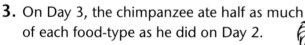

_____

_____

Show the data as a pie chart to check your answer.

Day 3	Kilograms
Fruit	1.475
Birds' eggs	
Small animals	
Insects	
Plant matter	

NOW TRY THIS!

Plant matter includes bark, blossom, leaves, seeds, and so on.

During the months of May to August, about one-third of the chimp's diet is seeds.

During January and February, about 90% of the chimp's diet is fruit.

From September to December, about half the chimp's diet is insects.

• Write a report about the eating habits of this chimpanzee, based on the figures for Days 1, 2 and 3. Explain in which month of the year you think the survey might have taken place.

A **pie chart** is a circle divided into sectors so that the areas of the sectors represent the data. To estimate fractions of a pie chart, it is useful to imagine the pie split into equal sectors (for example, if you imagine it split into five equal sectors, each sector is one-fifth, or 20%, of the whole).

Blockbuster!

A At a multi-screen cinema, the latest blockbuster film is showing every two hours. This bar chart shows the number of people in the audience for each start time on one Thursday in June.

MAN at BLACKS

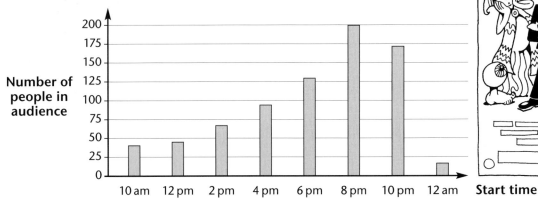

1. Estimate how many people went to see the film at:

(a) 10 am _____   (b) 4 pm _____   (c) 6 pm _____   (d) 8 pm _____

2. About how many more people saw the film at 12 pm than at 12 am? _____

3. About how many fewer people saw the film at 10 am than at 10 pm? _____

4. Approximately how many people saw the film in total? _____

5.   Look at this price list.

(a) About how many people paid the more expensive price? _____

Price list
£5.50 for 6 pm, 8 pm, 10 pm showings
£4.50 for all other showings

(b) About how many people paid the cheaper price? _____

(c) Approximately how much money in total did the cinema receive from people seeing the film on this day? _____

B 1. This table shows the number of people at each showing on Saturday of the same week.

On the graph above, draw bars in a different colour to show this data. Draw a key.

Answer question 5 above, for the new data.

(a) _____   (b) _____   (c) _____

2. Write a description comparing the data for Thursday and Saturday. Give possible reasons for the differences.

Start time	People
10 am	42
12 pm	68
2 pm	110
4 pm	150
6 pm	183
8 pm	180
10 pm	180
12 am	94

_____

_____

_____

When you read a graph or chart, look carefully at the scale. You could draw extra marks along the scale to help you read the height of the bars more accurately.

Developing Numeracy
Handling Data
Year 7
© A & C BLACK

Blockbuster!

C At a multi-screen cinema, the latest blockbuster film is showing. This bar chart shows the amount of money paid for tickets for this film during one week.

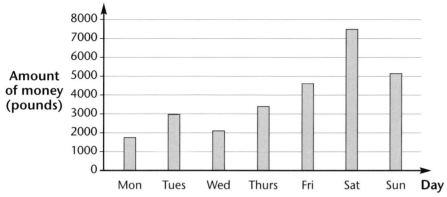

THE FINAL EPISODE (honest!)

1. **(a)** On which three days did the cinema receive the most money from the film?

   _____

   (b) Why might this be? _____

2. Approximately how much money did the cinema receive for this film:

   (a) on these three days? _____ **(b)** in total for the whole week? _____

3. About what fraction of the total for the whole week did the cinema receive on these

   three days? _____

4. It costs the cinema £1200 per day to show the film.

   (a) On the graph above, draw bars to show the ⟨profit⟩ the cinema made each day.
   Use a different colour for these bars and draw a key.

   (b) On which days did the cinema make about £2000 profit? _____

5. During the following week, it costs only £800 per day
   to show the film. This table shows the **profit** for each day.

   Draw another bar chart. Draw bars to show the amount of
   money received each day and draw bars to show the profit.

	Profit (£)
Monday	1200
Tuesday	3000
Wednesday	2400
Thursday	3320
Friday	4100
Saturday	7000
Sunday	6400

6. Write a description comparing the two sets of data.
   Give possible reasons for the differences.

   _____

   _____

   _____

NOW TRY THIS!

- 🖩 Find the approximate total amount of money received by the cinema for both weeks.
- 🖩 If the ticket price was £5, about how many people saw the film during those
  two weeks?

 When you read a graph or chart, look carefully at the scale. You could draw extra marks along the scale to help you read the height of the bars more accurately. To find the **profit**, subtract the amount of money it costs to show the film from the amount of money received in ticket sales.

Puffin – or just out of breath?

A

This bar chart shows the number of puffins (in thousands) breeding on a Welsh island between the years 1990 and 2003.

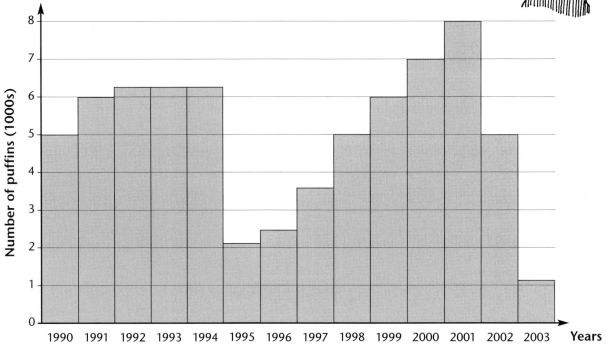

1. Estimate how many puffins bred in:

(a) 1994 _____ **(b)** 1995 _____ **(c)** 1998 _____ **(d)** 2001 _____

2. During which year (or years) was the approximate number of breeding puffins:

(a) about 2000? _____ **(b)** about 5000? _____

(c) about 6000? _____ **(d)** about 8000? _____

B

1. In which three **consecutive** years was the number of breeding puffins about the same?

_____

2. What happened to the puffin numbers during the years:

(a) 1995 to 2001? _____

(b) 1994 to 1995? _____

3. What difference do you notice between the way puffin numbers rise and the way they fall?

_____

4. Think about things that could affect the numbers of puffins breeding on this Welsh island.

What might have caused the fall in numbers from 2001 to 2003? _____

Look carefully at the scale on the bar chart and make sure you understand what each axis is showing. **Consecutive** years come one after the other.

Developing Numeracy
Handling Data
Year 7
© A & C BLACK

Puffin – or just out of breath?

C This bar chart shows the number of puffins (in thousands) breeding on a Welsh island between the years 1990 and 2003.

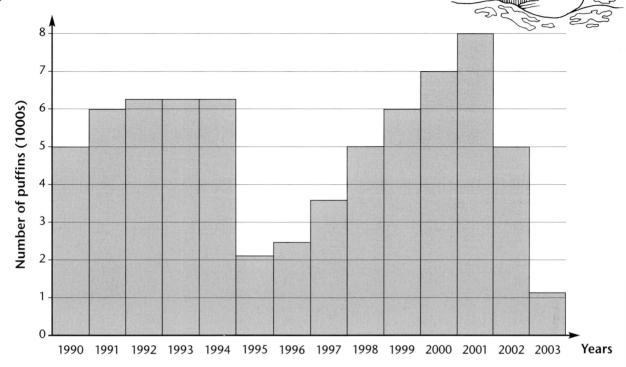

1. Look at the puffin numbers. Between which two years was there:

   (a) the largest increase? _____   **(b)** the largest decrease? _____

   (c) the smallest increase? _____   **(d)** the smallest decrease? _____

2. About how many more puffins bred in:

   (a) 2002 than 1996? _____   **(b)** 2000 than 1997? _____

   > Puffins tend to starve in cold winters because their food is scarce. When food is plentiful their numbers rise steadily. Their food (fish) is plentiful during warm weather. If the winter is mild, puffin numbers remain about the same.

3. Write what you think the weather was like during:

   (a) 1990–1991 _____   **(b)** 2002–2003 _____

   _____   _____

   _____   _____

   _____   _____

NOW TRY THIS!

- Draw a bar chart to show how you think puffin numbers would change if the years:

  2003, 2004 and 2009 had mild winters
  2005 and 2010 had very cold winters
  2006 and 2007 were warm throughout
  2008 and 2011 had quite cold winters

Look carefully at the scale on the bar chart and make sure you understand what each axis is showing.

Developing Numeracy
Handling Data
Year 7
© A & C BLACK

33

Chocaholics

A

This table shows the number of boxes of chocolates (in thousands) sold during each quarter of 2003 for four chocolate manufacturers.

	1st quarter	2nd quarter	3rd quarter	4th quarter	Total
D-lite	11	25	17	26	79
N-tice	7	28	14	22	
U-phoric	22	21	26	55	
X-cite	8	14	36	28	

1. Fill in the **total** column to show the number of boxes of chocolates (in thousands) each firm sold in 2003.

2. Which firm sold the most boxes:

   (a) in the 1st quarter? _____   **(b)** in the 3rd quarter? _____

   (c) in the 4th quarter? _____   **(d)** in total? _____

3. **(a)** In which quarter were most boxes sold? _____

   (b) Why do you think this is? _____

   _____

4. **(a)** Give possible reasons why X-cite's sales went up so much in the 3rd quarter.

   _____

   _____

   (b) What was the effect of this on the sales figures of the other firms?

   _____

5. What type of graph or chart would most clearly show whether U-phoric sold over one-third of all the boxes sold? _____

B

1. Key the data from the totals column into a spreadsheet of a data handling program. Show it as a **pie chart**.

2. Approximately what **percentage** of all the boxes sold were:

   (a) D-lite? _____   **(b)** U-phoric? _____

3. Approximately what **fraction** of all the boxes sold were:

   (a) N-tice? _____   **(b)** X-cite? _____

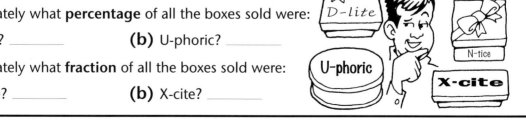

A **pie chart** is a circle divided into sectors so that the areas of the sectors represent the data. When you estimate a percentage of a pie chart, remember that the whole is 100%, half is 50%, and so on. To estimate fractions, it is useful to imagine the pie split into equal sectors (for example, if it is split into five equal sectors, each sector is one-fifth, or 20%).

Developing Numeracy
Handling Data
Year 7
© A & C BLACK

Chocaholics

This table shows the number of boxes of chocolates (in thousands) sold during each quarter of 2003 for four chocolate manufacturers.

	1st quarter	2nd quarter	3rd quarter	4th quarter	Total
D-lite	11	25	17	26	79
N-tice	7	28	14	22	
U-phoric	22	21	26	55	
X-cite	8	14	36	28	

1. **(a)** Fill in the total number of boxes sold (in thousands) by each firm.

   (b) How many boxes were sold altogether during the year? _____

2. On a pie chart, this total will be represented by 360°.

   (a) How many degrees will be the sector representing 79 thousand boxes? _____

   (b) Use a protractor to draw a pie chart. Show the proportion of boxes of chocolates sold by each firm during the year.

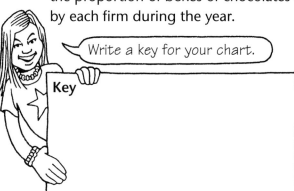

Write a key for your chart.

Key

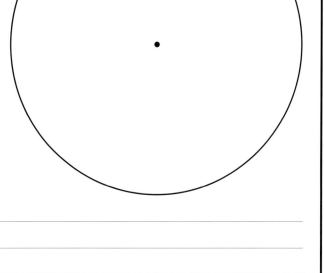

   (c) Write four statements about the proportion of the total number of boxes of chocolates sold by each firm.

   _____

   _____

   _____

   _____

NOW TRY THIS!

This table shows the **mean** number of boxes sold per quarter in 2002.

- 🖩 Find the mean number of boxes sold per quarter in 2003. Complete the table.
- Describe whether each firm had a better year in 2003 than in 2002.

	2002	2003
D-lite	20	
N-tice	23.25	
U-phoric	27	
X-cite	20.5	

Remember that the total number of boxes is represented by 360° in the pie chart. Use division to find out how many boxes each degree will represent, or how many degrees each thousand boxes will require. The **mean** number of boxes sold per quarter is the total number of boxes sold in the year divided by four (the number of quarters).

Developing Numeracy
Handling Data
Year 7
© A & C BLACK

35

Pie in the sky

A Each day at midday, a weather station records the level of cloud cover in the sky.
This **pie chart** shows the different levels of cloud cover during one month.

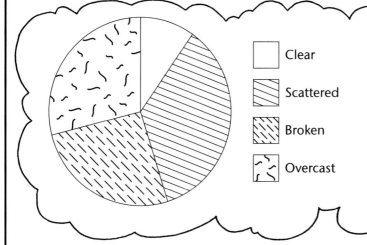

☐ Clear

▨ Scattered

▨ Broken

▨ Overcast

Clear – the sky has no clouds, or clouds cover less than $\frac{1}{10}$ of the sky.

Scattered – an average of $\frac{1}{10}$ to $\frac{5}{10}$ of the sky is covered with clouds.

Broken – an average of $\frac{5}{10}$ to $\frac{9}{10}$ of the sky is covered with clouds.

Overcast – more than $\frac{9}{10}$ of the sky is covered with clouds.

1. Approximately what **fraction** of the days this month had:

(a) broken cloud cover? _____

(b) overcast cloud cover? _____

(c) less than 10% of cloud cover? _____

(d) scattered cloud cover? _____

2. Do you think this month is in spring, summer, autumn or winter, or is it impossible to say?

3. Can you tell from the pie chart how many days are in this month? _____

4. Approximately how many days in this month had:

(a) broken cloud cover? _____

(b) overcast cloud cover? _____

(c) less than 10% of cloud cover? _____

(d) scattered cloud cover? _____

B This bar chart shows cloud cover information for a different month.

(a) Which season do you think this might be?

_____

(b) How many days are in this month? _____

(c) Do you think there were more days this month with scattered clouds than for the month shown in the pie chart? Explain your answer.

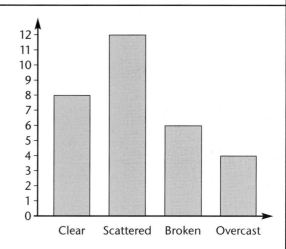

_____

_____

A **pie chart** is a circle divided into sectors so that the areas of the sectors represent the data. When you estimate a percentage of a pie chart, remember that the whole is 100%, half is 50%, and so on. To estimate fractions, it is useful to imagine the pie split into equal sectors (for example, if it is split into five equal sectors, each sector is one-fifth, or 20%).

Developing Numeracy
Handling Data
Year 7
© A & C BLACK

Pie in the sky

Two airlines each produce a **pie chart** to show what proportion of their flights go to different continents.

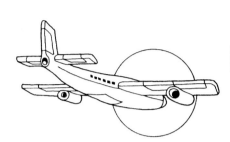

FlyFar airlines

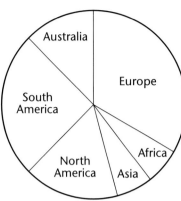

FlyCheap airlines

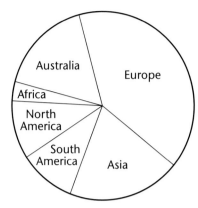

1. Approximately what **fraction** of the FlyFar flights go to:

(a) Europe? _____ **(b)** North America? _____ **(c)** Africa? _____

(d) Asia? _____ **(e)** South America? _____ **(f)** Australia? _____

2. Approximately what **percentage** of the FlyCheap flights go to:

(a) Europe? _____ **(b)** North America? _____ **(c)** Africa? _____

(d) Asia? _____ **(e)** South America? _____ **(f)** Australia? _____

3. Are these statements true? For each one, write **true**, **false** or **can't tell**.

(a) FlyFar has more flights to Europe than FlyCheap. _____

(b) FlyFar has more flights to Europe than to Asia. _____

(c) FlyFar has over 50% more flights to Europe than to Africa. _____

(d) FlyCheap has more flights to Australia than FlyFar. _____

(e) FlyCheap has fewer flights to North and South America than to Asia. _____

(f) FlyCheap has about three times as many flights to Europe as to South America. _____

4. Discuss your answers with a partner.

NOW TRY THIS!

● If FlyFar has 10 000 flights a year and FlyCheap has 15 000, estimate who has the most flights to:

(a) Europe _____ **(b)** North America _____ **(c)** Africa _____

(d) Asia _____ **(e)** South America _____ **(f)** Australia _____

A **pie chart** is a circle divided into sectors so that the areas of the sectors represent the data. When you estimate a percentage of a pie chart, remember that the whole is 100%, half is 50%, and so on. To estimate fractions, it is useful to imagine the pie split into equal sectors (for example, if it is split into five equal sectors, each sector is one-fifth, or 20%).

A question of sport

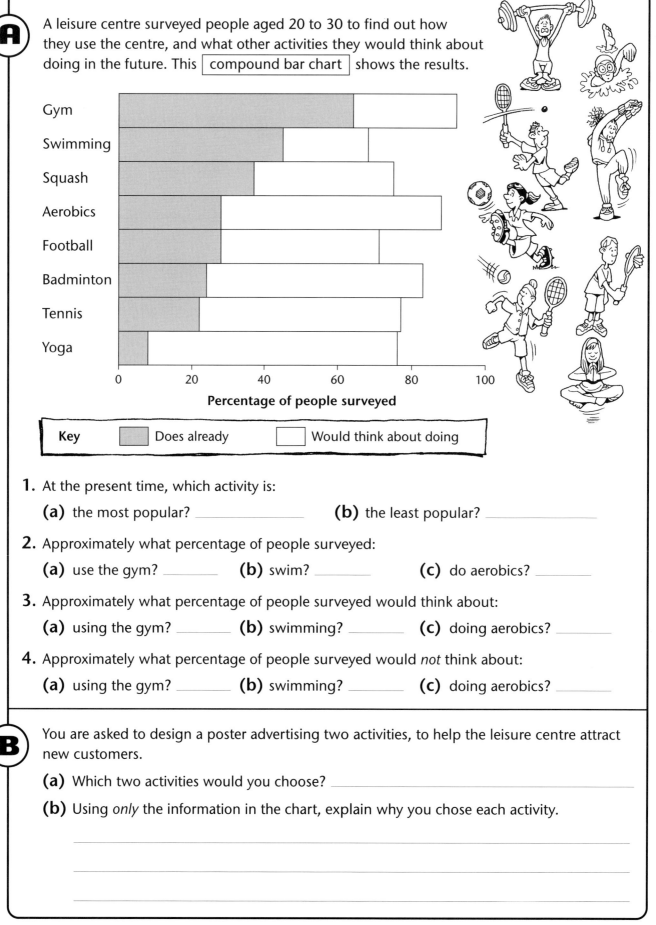

A A leisure centre surveyed people aged 20 to 30 to find out how they use the centre, and what other activities they would think about doing in the future. This | compound bar chart | shows the results.

Key ▨ Does already   ☐ Would think about doing

1. At the present time, which activity is:

   (a) the most popular? _____   **(b)** the least popular? _____

2. Approximately what percentage of people surveyed:

   (a) use the gym? _____   **(b)** swim? _____   **(c)** do aerobics? _____

3. Approximately what percentage of people surveyed would think about:

   (a) using the gym? _____   **(b)** swimming? _____   **(c)** doing aerobics? _____

4. Approximately what percentage of people surveyed would *not* think about:

   (a) using the gym? _____   **(b)** swimming? _____   **(c)** doing aerobics? _____

B You are asked to design a poster advertising two activities, to help the leisure centre attract new customers.

   (a) Which two activities would you choose? _____

   (b) Using *only* the information in the chart, explain why you chose each activity.

   _____

   _____

   _____

A **compound bar chart** shows two sets of information at the same time. One part of a bar represents one thing, and the other part represents something else.

Developing Numeracy
Handling Data
Year 7
© A & C BLACK

A question of sport

C A leisure centre surveyed the views of people aged 10 to 19 who use the centre. Here are the results.

	Activities at the centre that:	
	I do now (%)	I would think about doing (%)
Gym	21	15
Swimming	38	23
Squash	10	45
Aerobics	24	15
Football	37	47
Badminton	28	34
Tennis	16	52
Yoga	8	12

1. Draw a **compound bar chart** to show this information. Write a key for your chart.

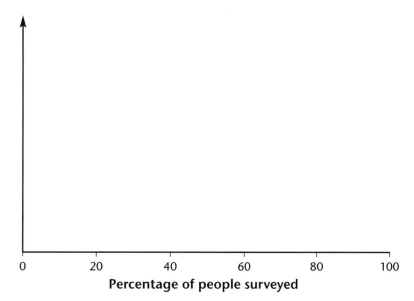

Percentage of people surveyed

Key ☐   ☐

2. What percentage of people surveyed would *not* think about:

(a) using the gym? _____

(b) swimming? _____

(c) playing squash? _____

(d) doing aerobics? _____

(e) playing football? _____

(f) playing badminton? _____

(g) playing tennis? _____

(h) doing yoga? _____

NOW TRY THIS!
- List the names of eight singers, pop groups or bands. For each one, ask ten friends whether:
  (a) they have bought a CD by the artist(s)
  (b) they would consider buying a CD by the artist(s).
- Draw a compound bar chart to show this information.

 A **compound bar chart** shows two sets of information at the same time. One part of a bar represents one thing, and the other part represents something else.

Interpret charts and draw conclusions

Car trouble

A A survey found out what percentage of five-year-old cars broke down in the past 12 months. These are the results for different makes.

Number of people who took part in the survey for each make of car.

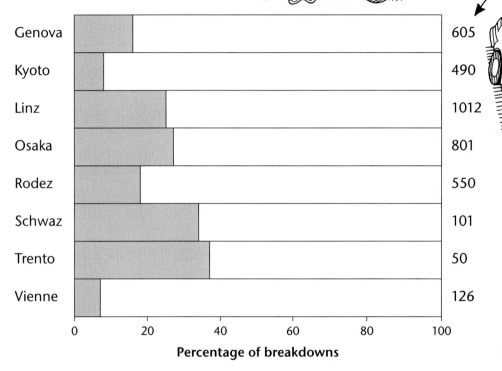

Genova	605
Kyoto	490
Linz	1012
Osaka	801
Rodez	550
Schwaz	101
Trento	50
Vienne	126

Percentage of breakdowns

1. Approximately what **percentage** of these makes of car broke down?

    (a) Kyoto _____   **(b)** Rodez _____   **(c)** Osaka _____   **(d)** Trento _____

2. Approximately what **fraction** of these makes of car broke down?

    (a) Kyoto _____   **(b)** Rodez _____   **(c)** Osaka _____   **(d)** Trento _____

3. Approximately what **percentage** of these makes of car did *not* break down?

    (a) Linz _____   **(b)** Vienne _____   **(c)** Schwaz _____   **(d)** Genova _____

B

1. Approximately **how many** of these makes of car broke down?

    (a) Osaka *about $\frac{1}{4}$ of 800 =* _____   **(b)** Rodez _____

    (c) Kyoto _____   **(d)** Trento _____

    (e) Schwaz _____   **(f)** Linz _____

2. Approximately **how many** of these makes of car did *not* break down?

    (a) Osaka *about $\frac{3}{4}$ of 800 =* _____   **(b)** Rodez _____

    (c) Kyoto _____   **(d)** Trento _____

    (e) Schwaz _____   **(f)** Linz _____

3. Does the survey show more Trento breakdowns or more Linz breakdowns? _____

To find the percentage of cars that did *not* break down, subtract the percentage of cars that did break down from 100%.

Developing Numeracy
Handling Data
Year 7
© A & C BLACK

40

Car trouble

A survey found out what percentage of two-year-old cars broke down in the past 12 months. These are the results for different makes.

Number of people who took part in the survey for each make of car.

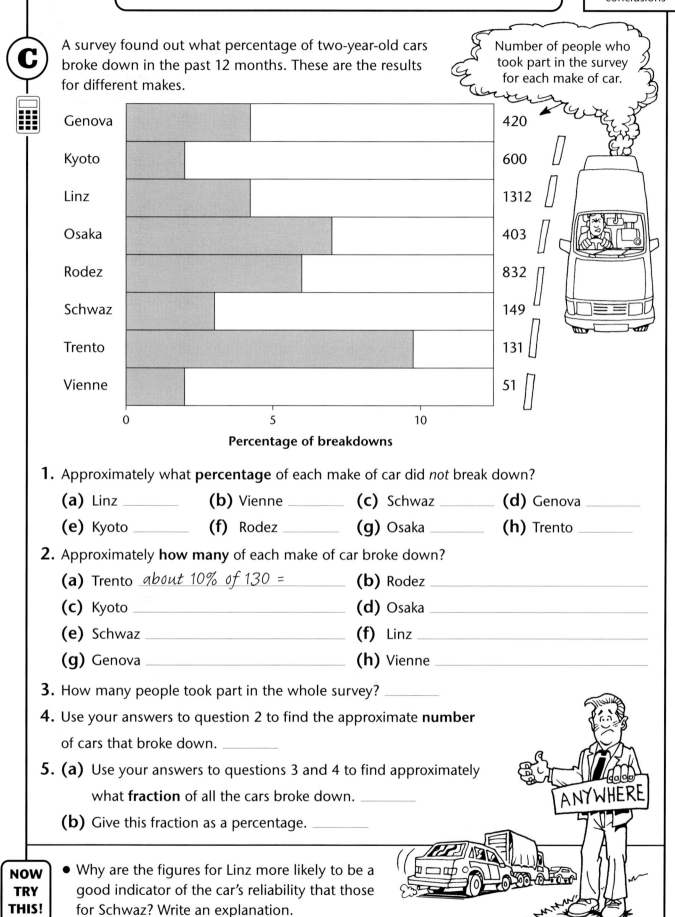

Percentage of breakdowns

Make	Number
Genova	420
Kyoto	600
Linz	1312
Osaka	403
Rodez	832
Schwaz	149
Trento	131
Vienne	51

1. Approximately what **percentage** of each make of car did *not* break down?

   (a) Linz _____ **(b)** Vienne _____ **(c)** Schwaz _____ **(d)** Genova _____

   (e) Kyoto _____ **(f)** Rodez _____ **(g)** Osaka _____ **(h)** Trento _____

2. Approximately **how many** of each make of car broke down?

   (a) Trento *about 10% of 130 =* _____ **(b)** Rodez _____

   (c) Kyoto _____ **(d)** Osaka _____

   (e) Schwaz _____ **(f)** Linz _____

   (g) Genova _____ **(h)** Vienne _____

3. How many people took part in the whole survey? _____

4. Use your answers to question 2 to find the approximate **number** of cars that broke down. _____

5. **(a)** Use your answers to questions 3 and 4 to find approximately what **fraction** of all the cars broke down. _____

   (b) Give this fraction as a percentage. _____

NOW TRY THIS!

• Why are the figures for Linz more likely to be a good indicator of the car's reliability that those for Schwaz? Write an explanation.

To find the percentage of cars that did *not* break down, subtract the percentage of cars that did break down from 100%.

Puppy power

These diagrams show the different types of averages (mode, median and mean). The bars represent the heights of five puppies.

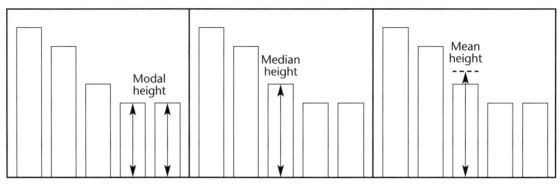

The **mode** (or **modal height**) is the most common height.

The **median** is the height of the puppy in the middle when they are arranged in order.

The **mean** is the height found by adding the heights together and dividing by the number of puppies.

This list shows the number of puppies in 11 Pekinese litters.

| 1, | 1, | 4, | 3, | 2, | 5, | 6, | 2, | 3, | 4, | 1 |

(a) Find the **modal number** of pups per litter. _____

(b) Find the **median** number of pups per litter. _____

(c) Find the **mean** number of pups per litter (to 1 d.p.). _____

(d) Discuss with a partner which of the three averages you think is most useful in describing the number of puppies per litter.

B

The lists below show the number of puppies in the litters of two breeds of dog.

| **Border Collie** | 4, | 5, | 7, | 8, | 7, | 5, | 7, | 6, | 6, | 7, | 5 |
| **Poodle** | 3, | 5, | 9, | 6, | 7, | 6, | 6, | 8, | 5, | 4, | 8 |

1. For each breed, find the **mean** number of pups per litter (to 1 d.p.). Then find the **range**.

	Border Collie	**Poodle**
Mean		
Range		

To find the range, subtract the lowest value from the highest value.

!

2. Write a description comparing the number of puppies per litter for these two breeds.

_____

_____

_____

If two (or more) values are the most common, they should both be given as the mode.

Developing Numeracy
Handling Data
Year 7
© A & C BLACK

Puppy power

C These tables show the number of puppies in the litters of three breeds of dog. Fifty litters of each breed were surveyed.

German Shepherd

Number of pups per litter	4	5	6	7	8	9	10	11	12	13	14	15+
Number of litters	0	1	4	12	10	10	8	2	2	1	0	0

Labrador

Number of pups per litter	4	5	6	7	8	9	10	11	12	13	14	15+
Number of litters	2	2	4	8	11	10	7	3	1	1	1	0

Airedale Terrier

Number of pups per litter	4	5	6	7	8	9	10	11	12	13	14	15+
Number of litters	0	5	11	17	10	4	3	0	0	0	0	0

1. (a) Find the **modal number** of pups per litter.

German Shepherd _____   Labrador _____   Airedale Terrier _____

(b) Find the **range**.

German Shepherd _____   Labrador _____   Airedale Terrier _____

(c) Write a description comparing the number of puppies per litter for these three breeds.

_____

_____

_____

_____

2. German Shepherd dogs weigh more than Labradors, and Labradors weigh more than Airedale Terriers. Do you agree with the statement below?

> **Heavier breeds of dog tend to have a higher average number of puppies per litter.**

Explain your answer, using the information in the tables.

_____

_____

• Describe the litter sizes of these two dog breeds. Compare them with those above. The **mean** and the **range** is shown.

Find the mean for each dog breed above.

King Charles Spaniel

Mean litter size 4.1
Range 5

Red Setter

Mean litter size 7.6
Range 9

 Remember, the **mode** or **modal value** is the most common or popular value. If two (or more) values are the most popular, they should both be given as the mode. To find the **range**, subtract the lowest value from the highest value. The **mean** is the total number of puppies divided by the total number of litters.

In a word

A

This newspaper article, including the title, is 100 words long.

SOW ON

Get seeds on the grow now

Growing your own plants from seed is not only good value, it is also immensely satisfying.

Now is a good time to start sowing many flowering plants for your garden, giving some of the slower annuals and even some herbaceous perennials a head start.

Many herbaceous perennials, if sown this early, will produce a fair show of flowers later. It really helps if you have a heated propagator.

You will also need some clean seed trays (I prefer the smallest sizes as I rarely want a quantity of one variety of plant).

(a) Count the number of words with one and two letters. Complete the second row of the frequency table. Check that this row totals 100 words.

Number of letters per word	1	2	3	4	5	6	7	8	9	10	11+	Total
Number of words	___	___	14	28	11	10	5	2	2	6	0	100
Total letters			42									

(3 × 14)

Mean = _____

(b) Fill in the last row of the table by multiplying the values in the rows above.

(c) Now find the total number of letters by adding all the numbers in the last row.

(d) Find the **mean** number of letters per word for this article.

B

This week's checklist

Conservatory and glasshouse plant care

Plan watering times carefully. If done in the morning the plant has more hours to absorb moisture and an opportunity to dry out a little. Watering in late afternoon may leave it unnecessarily sitting in damp conditions overnight.

Ensuring good practice like this in the conservatory and greenhouse will help to protect plants from botrytis. This can spread incredibly rapidly in warm, humid conditions and appears as a fuzzy, grey fungal growth on leaves and stems. To stop the disease spreading, clear up dead and dying material and space plants further apart.

1. Complete the table for this 100-word article. Find the mean number of letters per word.

Number of letters per word	1	2	3	4	5	6	7	8	9	10	11	12	13	14+	Total
Number of words	___	___	16	18	13	8	7	7	5	5	1	2	1	0	100
Total letters															

Mean = _____

2. For each newspaper article, find the **range** of the data. Compare the two articles using the mean and range. Discuss your answers with a partner.

To find the **mean** number of letters per word, you first need to multiply the values in the frequency table. Find the total number of letters and divide it by the total number of words to give the mean. Remember, you can find the **range** by subtracting the lowest value from the highest value.

In a word

C Your teacher will give you a page from a newspaper.

1. **(a)** Write the name of the newspaper here: _____

   (b) Choose any section and draw a box around the first 100 words.

   (c) Find the word with the most letters. _____ It has _____ letters.

   (d) Find the word with the fewest letters. _____ It has _____ letter(s).

   (e) What is the **range**? _____

2. Now draw a frequency table to record the number of words of different lengths.

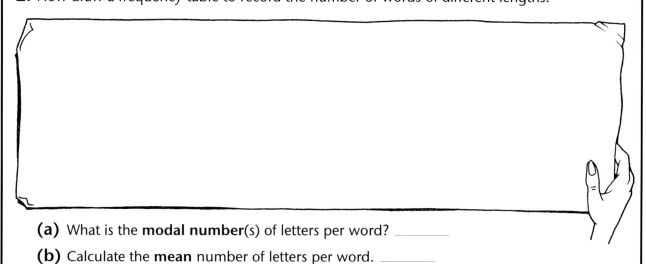

   (a) What is the **modal number**(s) of letters per word? _____

   (b) Calculate the **mean** number of letters per word. _____

3. Ask four pupils with different newspapers to give you their **range** and **mean**. Fill in this table.

Newspaper	Range	Mean

4. Now write a description, comparing the lengths of the words in different newspapers.

   _____

   _____

   _____

   _____

NOW TRY THIS!

- Record which of the newspapers are tabloids and which are broadsheets.
- Can you make any generalisations about the lengths of the words in these two types of newspaper? Explain your answer.

 Remember, you can find the **range** by subtracting the lowest value from the highest value. The **mode** or **modal value** is the most common or popular value. To find the **mean** number of letters per word, you first need to multiply the values in the frequency table. Find the total number of letters and divide it by the total number of words to give the mean.

Developing Numeracy
Handling Data
Year 7
© A & C BLACK

Be a reporter

A This newspaper report is about the increase in passenger numbers at UK airports. Use the graph to help you fill in the blanks.

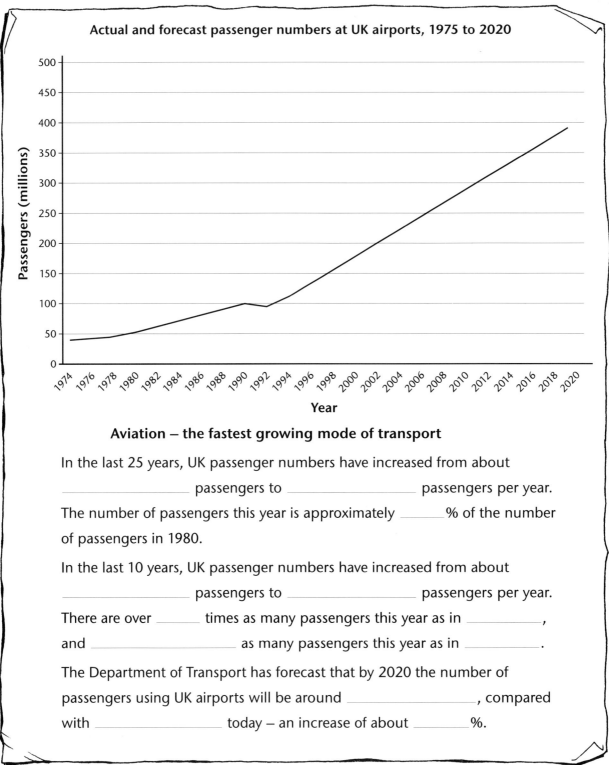

Actual and forecast passenger numbers at UK airports, 1975 to 2020

Passengers (millions)

Year

Aviation – the fastest growing mode of transport

In the last 25 years, UK passenger numbers have increased from about _____ passengers to _____ passengers per year.

The number of passengers this year is approximately _____% of the number of passengers in 1980.

In the last 10 years, UK passenger numbers have increased from about _____ passengers to _____ passengers per year.

There are over _____ times as many passengers this year as in _____, and _____ as many passengers this year as in _____.

The Department of Transport has forecast that by 2020 the number of passengers using UK airports will be around _____, compared with _____ today – an increase of about _____%.

B On a separate piece of paper, write a more detailed report. Suggest reasons for the rise in passenger numbers and what the effects of increased air traffic might be. Include other information from the graph.

 To find what percentage this year's figure is of the 1980 figure, see roughly how many million passengers there are this year and divide this number by 50 (because 50 million was the approximate number of passengers in 1980). Then multiply this by 100 to give a percentage.

Developing Numeracy
Handling Data
Year 7
© A & C BLACK

Be a reporter

C Work with a partner to answer this question:

> **In football matches, are more goals scored in the first 15 minutes of each half than in the last 15 minutes of each half?**

Think carefully about how you might find the answer to the question.
Here are some things to consider:

First, do I understand the question?

What do I predict the answer will be?

Where can I find this sort of data?

Will I look only at Premiership matches?

How much data shall I collect?

What kind of table shall I draw?

Shall I group the data?

Are one week's results sufficient?

Collect the data and write a newspaper report about your findings. Use as much data as you can in your report. Include other interesting things you found out.

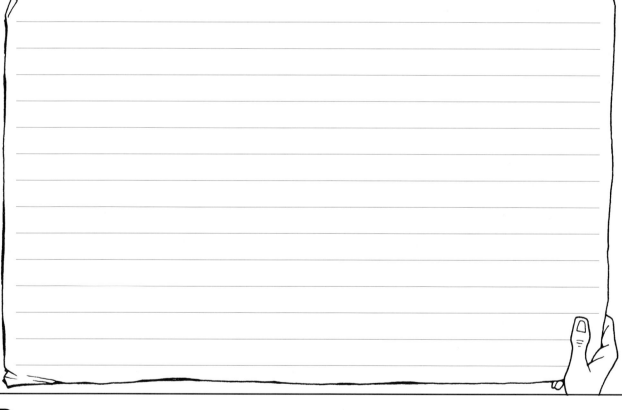

NOW TRY THIS!

- Group the information you collected in a different way, to answer this question:

> **In football matches, are more goals scored in the first 8 minutes of each half than in the last 8 minutes of each half?**

Remember, the more data you collect, the more accurate the results will be.

What are the chances?

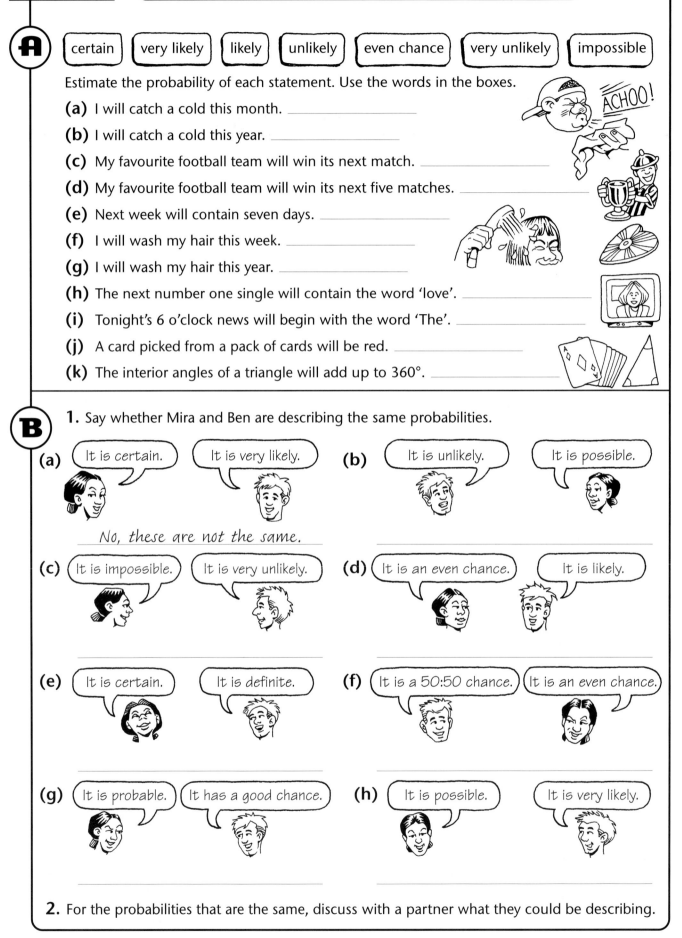

A

certain | very likely | likely | unlikely | even chance | very unlikely | impossible

Estimate the probability of each statement. Use the words in the boxes.

(a) I will catch a cold this month. _____

(b) I will catch a cold this year. _____

(c) My favourite football team will win its next match. _____

(d) My favourite football team will win its next five matches. _____

(e) Next week will contain seven days. _____

(f) I will wash my hair this week. _____

(g) I will wash my hair this year. _____

(h) The next number one single will contain the word 'love'. _____

(i) Tonight's 6 o'clock news will begin with the word 'The'. _____

(j) A card picked from a pack of cards will be red. _____

(k) The interior angles of a triangle will add up to 360°. _____

B

1. Say whether Mira and Ben are describing the same probabilities.

(a) It is certain. / It is very likely.

No, these are not the same.

(b) It is unlikely. / It is possible.

_____

(c) It is impossible. / It is very unlikely.

_____

(d) It is an even chance. / It is likely.

_____

(e) It is certain. / It is definite.

_____

(f) It is a 50:50 chance. / It is an even chance.

_____

(g) It is probable. / It has a good chance.

_____

(h) It is possible. / It is very likely.

_____

2. For the probabilities that are the same, discuss with a partner what they could be describing.

 Many different words are used to describe probabilities: for example, likely, possible, probable. Use a dictionary if you are not sure what they mean.

Developing Numeracy
Handling Data
Year 7
© A & C BLACK

What are the chances?

C

1. Use the words on the door to describe the probability of the next person entering your classroom being:

Explain your answers.

certain, probable, likely, very unlikely, impossible, very likely, even chance, possible, fair chance, unlikely, poor chance

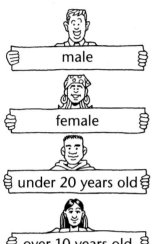

male

female

under 20 years old

over 10 years old

in spectacles

in a jumper

known to you

a teacher

a policeman

a Martian

2. Compare and discuss your answers with a partner.

NOW TRY THIS!

- Look again at the probability words at the top of the page. List them in order of likelihood, from **certain** to **impossible**.
- Compare and discuss your list with a partner.

IMPOSSIBLE

To describe these probabilities, you need to think about the people in your school: for example, are there more males than females?

**Developing Numeracy
Handling Data
Year 7
© A & C BLACK**

49

Find the outcomes

A Tick the events that have two or more equally likely outcomes. Next to each tick, write how many equally likely outcomes the situation has.

(a) rolling a dice

✔ 6

(b) picking a playing card at random from a pack

☐ _____

(c) tossing a coin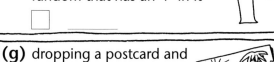

☐ _____

(d) dropping a plastic cup and it landing upside down

☐ _____

(e) choosing a month of the year at random that has an 'r' in it *r*

☐ _____

(f) picking a playing card from a pack and getting a picture card

☐ _____

(g) dropping a postcard and it landing picture side up

☐ _____

(h) choosing a letter of the alphabet at random and getting a vowel

a, b, c, d, e, f, g...

☐ _____

(i) a new baby being a girl or a boy

☐ _____

(j) choosing a day of the week at random that ends in 'y' *y*

☐ _____

B **1.** What are the probabilities of rolling each of these numbers on this spinner? Write your answers as fractions.

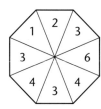

(a) 1 $\frac{1}{8}$

(b) 2 _____

(c) 3 _____

(d) 4 _____

(e) 5 _____

(f) 6 _____

2. Explain your answer to question 1(c). _____

_____

3. Mark the fractions on this probability scale.

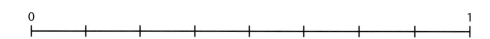

0   1

4. The table shows the probability of rolling each number on a different spinner. Fill in the numbers on the spinner.

Number	Probability
1	$\frac{1}{4}$
2	0
3	$\frac{1}{8}$
4	0
5	$\frac{3}{8}$
6	$\frac{1}{4}$

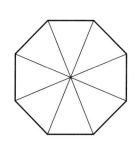

 Equally likely outcomes means that all of the possible results of an event (like rolling a dice) are equally likely to happen. When you roll a dice, you can get a 1, 2, 3, 4, 5 or 6. So there are six possible outcomes and they are all equally likely. Remember that there are 52 cards in a pack.

Developing Numeracy
Handling Data
Year 7
© A & C BLACK

50

Find the outcomes

1. The letters in the word PARALLEL are written on cards and put into a bag. One card will be picked at random.

   (a) When you pick a **card**, how many possible outcomes are there? _____

   (b) When you pick a **card**, are all the possible outcomes equally likely? _____

   Explain your answer. _____

   _____

   (c) What would be the probability of choosing each **letter** at random? Write your answers as fractions.

	A	E	L	P	R

   Probability:

2. These eight teams are in the quarter-finals of the Cup. Their names are drawn one by one from a bag, at random.

Arsenal	Liverpool
Derby County	Manchester United
Leeds United	Leicester City
Southampton	Oxford United

   Write the probability of the first club drawn from the bag:

   (a) being Arsenal $\frac{1}{8}$

   (b) beginning with a vowel _____

   (c) beginning with 'L' _____

   (d) ending with 'd' _____

   (e) containing a 'p' _____

   (f) containing an 'a' _____

   (g) consisting of two words _____

   (h) having an odd number of letters _____

   (i) beginning and ending with the same letter _____

   (j) containing two consecutive letters in the same sequence as they appear in the alphabet, such as 'ab' _____

   (k) containing 11 letters _____

   (l) containing 12 letters _____

   Discuss your answers with a partner.

   • Write eight different probability questions for a partner to solve. You must work out the answers too!

 Equally likely outcomes means that all of the possible results of an event (like rolling a dice) are equally likely to happen. When you roll a dice, you can get a 1, 2, 3, 4, 5 or 6. So there are six possible outcomes and they are all equally likely.

How likely?

A Identify all the possible outcomes of these events. Describe each probability as a fraction and mark it on the probability scale.

Number of outcomes

(a) Event: a baby being born.
What is the probability of it being a boy?

0 ———————————— $\frac{1}{2}$ ———————————— 1

| 2 |

(b) Event: choosing a day at random.
What is the probability that it will begin with the letter 'T'?

0 ———————————————————————— 1

| |

(c) Event: rolling a dice.
What is the probability of getting a multiple of 2?

0 ———————————————————————— 1

| |

(d) Event: choosing a month at random.
What is the probability that it will contain the letter 'a'?

0 ———————————————————————— 1

| |

(e) Event: tossing a 1p and a 2p coin together.
What is the probability of getting two heads?

0 ———————————————————————— 1

| |

(f) Event: picking a card at random from a pack of cards.
What is the probability of getting a spade?

0 ———————————————————————— 1

| |

There are 4 suits, and
13 cards in each suit. **!**

(g) Event: picking a card at random from a pack of cards.
What is the probability of getting a king?

0 ———————————————————————— 1

| |

B Think of two events of your own and write probability questions. Mark the probabilities on the scales.

Event: _____

What is the probability _____?

0 ———————————————————————— 1

Event: _____

What is the probability _____?

0 ———————————————————————— 1

To mark a fraction on a probability scale, split the line into the number of
equal parts shown by the denominator (for example, $\frac{3}{8}$ needs a scale split
into eight equal parts).

How likely?

C At a grocer's, 2000 items passed through the checkout. This chart shows the number of each item sold.

Item	Number sold	Item	Number sold
Cheese (packs)	50	Apples	250
Crisps (bags)	200	Dark chocolate bars	50
Bread (loaves)	800	Milk (litres)	400
Milk chocolate bars	150	Bananas	100

> Give each answer as a fraction in its simplest form. **!**

1. What is the probability of an item, picked at random, being:

(a) cheese $\frac{50}{2000} = \frac{1}{40}$ (b) apples _____

(c) crisps _____   (d) dark chocolate bars _____

(e) bread _____   (f) milk _____

(g) milk chocolate bars _____   (h) bananas _____

(i) an item beginning with 'b' _____   (j) chocolate _____

(k) fruit _____   (l) bread or crisps _____

(m) neither milk nor bananas _____   (n) neither bread nor crisps _____

2. (a) What would each of these probabilities be if only half the number of each item had passed through the checkout? Explain your answer. _____

_____

_____

(b) What would each probability be if twice the number of each item had passed through the checkout? _____

3. What would each probability be if bread and milk were removed from the list?

(a) cheese _____   (b) apples _____

(c) crisps _____   (d) dark chocolate bars _____

(e) milk chocolate bars _____   (f) bananas _____

NOW TRY THIS!
- Draw a 20 cm probability scale on a piece of paper.
- On the scale, mark and label each probability from question 1.

 To mark a fraction on a probability scale, split the line into the number of equal parts shown by the denominator (for example, $\frac{3}{8}$ needs a scale split into eight equal parts).

Dicey situations

A

1. Identify all the possible totals that can be made from rolling two dice.

_____

_____

2. (a) What is the highest total that can be made? _____

(b) What is the lowest total that can be made? _____

B

1. Try this experiment. You need ten small counters and two dice.

☆ On the board below, put your counters in any arrangement on the 'dice totals' lines. You can put several counters on one number if you want.

☆ Roll two dice. If you have a counter on that total, remove it. If you have more than one counter on that total, only remove one of them.

☆ Keep rolling the dice. Record how many goes it takes to clear the board.

Dice totals

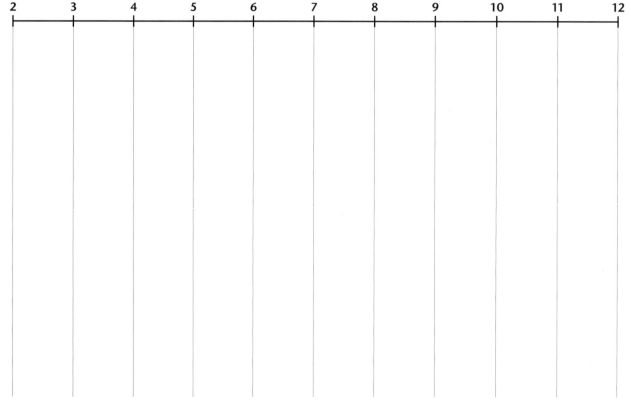

| 2 | 3 | 4 | 5 | 6 | 7 | 8 | 9 | 10 | 11 | 12 |

(a) Which totals tend to occur most often? _____

_____

(b) Why do you think this is? _____

_____

2. Replay the game several times, changing your arrangement each time. What have you found out about the likelihood of rolling different totals? Discuss this with a partner.

When you consider the likelihood of rolling different totals, think about the different ways you could roll a total of 7 with two dice. Then think about the number of different ways you could roll a total of 12.

**Developing Numeracy
Handling Data
Year 7**
© A & C BLACK

Dicey situations

1. Roll two dice. Record the outcome by putting a cross in a box beneath that total.
Continue until the crosses for one number reach the winning post.

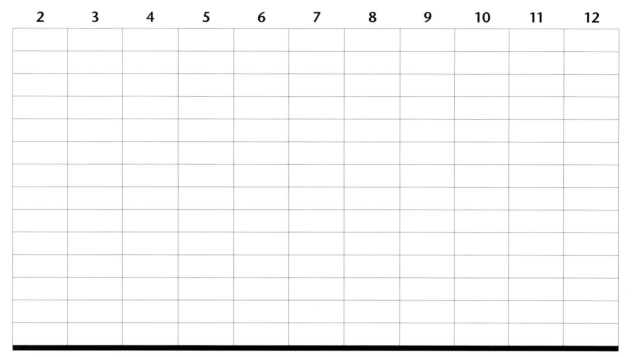

| 2 | 3 | 4 | 5 | 6 | 7 | 8 | 9 | 10 | 11 | 12 |

WINNING POST

(a) Which total reaches the winning post first? _____

(b) What do you think this result suggests? _____

_____

2. (a) Find out the winning totals of other pupils in your class.
Record them in the table below.

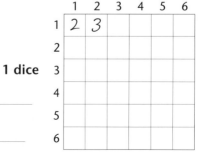

Winning totals	2	3	4	5	6	7	8	9	10	11	12
Number of pupils											

(b) What do these results suggest? _____

_____

NOW TRY THIS!

• Complete the grid to show all the possible outcomes of rolling two dice.

• Which total is most likely? _____

• What is the theoretical probability of:

(a) rolling a total of 7? _____   **(b)** rolling a total of 12? _____

(c) rolling a total of 4? _____   **(d)** rolling a total of 8? _____

1 dice

	1	2	3	4	5	6
1	2	3				
2						
3						
4						
5						
6						

1 dice

You can work out the **theoretical probability** if there are **equally likely
outcomes** (for example, if a dice is just as likely to fall on one number as
on any other). The more you do an experiment, the more likely you are to
get close to the theoretical probability.

Do an experiment

A

1. A coin can land head up (H) or tail up (T). When you toss two coins at the same time, there are four possible outcomes:

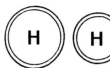 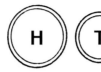  

What is the **theoretical probability** of getting:

(a) two heads? $\frac{1}{4}$ **(b)** one head and one tail? _____ **(c)** two tails? _____

2. About how many times would you expect two heads, if you tossed the coins:

(a) 10 times? _____ **(b)** 50 times? _____ **(c)** 100 times? _____

3. About how many times would you expect one head and one tail, if you tossed the coins:

(a) 10 times? _____ **(b)** 50 times? _____ **(c)** 100 times? _____

B

1. **(a)** Toss two coins together 20 times.
   Record your results in the grid below, like this:

(b) Fill in this table to show your results.

Outcomes	HH	HT	TH	TT
Frequency				

2. **(a)** Now repeat the experiment. Record your results below.

(b) Fill in this table to show your results.

Outcomes	HH	HT	TH	TT
Frequency				

(c) Were your results the same in both experiments? _____

3. What were the totals for each outcome from the **40** coin tosses altogether?

Outcomes	HH	HT	TH	TT
Frequency				

4. Now add your results to those of a partner.
   (a) What were the totals for each outcome from the **80** coin tosses altogether?

Outcomes	HH	HT	TH	TT
Frequency				

(b) Explain what you notice about the results. _____

 You can work out the **theoretical probability** if there are **equally likely outcomes** (for example, if a coin is just as likely to land head up as tail up). The more you do an experiment, the more likely you are to get close to the theoretical probability.

Developing Numeracy
Handling Data
Year 7
© A & C BLACK

Do an experiment

1. Play this game with a partner. You need two dice, and a copy of this sheet each.

☆ Roll both dice and record the total. Repeat again and again, adding your totals as you go. Stop whenever you want, because if you roll a total of 7, you lose all your score for that go.

☆ If you stop before you roll a total of 7, add your score to your running total. Then it's your partner's turn.

☆ If you roll a total of 7, write 'no score'. Play passes to your partner.

☆ The winner is the player with the highest running total after ten goes.

You can record your score like this:

Dice totals	Running total
8 + 9 + 10 + 4	31
5 + 11 + 7 no score	31

Dice totals	Running total	Dice totals	Running total

2. Discuss the strategies you used. How did you decide when to stop your go?

_____

_____

3. What is the probability of rolling a: **(a)** 7? _____ **(b)** 10? _____

4. Repeat the game using 10 as the 'no score' total.

(a) How did you change your strategy when the 'no score' total was 10? Explain why.

_____

_____

(b) Which 'no score' totals would enable you to get the highest running totals? Explain why.

_____

_____

NOW TRY THIS!

• Write a report about what you have discovered. Give an explanation of strategies to win the game for different 'no score' totals.

To find the probability of rolling a particular total, you first need to list all the different ways that each of the totals between 2 and 12 can be scored.

Probability test

A

1. Add pairs of these numbers in turn. Write down the totals.

> There are ten different pairs to add.

Totals	101									

2. Give the **theoretical probability** of each total if two numbers are chosen at random.

Total									
Probability									

> ☆ Write each number on a separate piece of paper.
> ☆ Choose a pair at random. Find and record the total.
> ☆ Repeat 30 times.

3. (a) How closely do your results match those from your table in question 2? Describe any differences. _____

_____

(b) Combine your results with those of a partner. Do the results match those from your table in question 2 more closely? _____

B

Liverpool Harriers   Feltham Spurs   Newcastle Harriers

Southampton Racers   Liverpool Flyers   Leeds Harriers

1. How many possible races could there be if two of these teams were picked at random to race each other? _____

2. If two teams were picked at random, what is the probability of:

(a) Liverpool Harriers racing Liverpool Flyers? _____

(b) Feltham Spurs racing a team from Liverpool? _____

(c) Southampton Racers racing a team with 'Harriers' in its name? _____

3. If Leeds Harriers were picked, what is the probability of Leeds racing against:

(a) Feltham Spurs? _____

(b) a team with 'Harriers' in its name? _____

(c) a team from Liverpool? _____

 You can work out the **theoretical probability** if there are **equally likely outcomes** (for example, if each number is just as likely to be picked as any other). The more you do an experiment, the more likely you are to get close to the theoretical probability.

Developing Numeracy
Handling Data
Year 7
© A & C BLACK

Probability test

C 1. (a) You need red, blue and green pencils.
Colour the three parts of each spinner in different colours.

Agree with a partner on which parts you will colour red, blue and green, so that your spinners are identical.

!

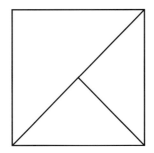 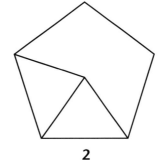 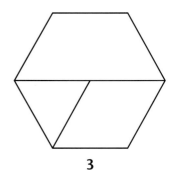

Spinner: 1   2   3

(b) For each spinner, write the **theoretical probability** of getting each colour.

Spinner	Red	Blue	Green
1			
2			
3			

(c) If you spun each spinner 20 times, about how many times would you expect to get each colour?

Spinner 1 R _____   B _____   G _____

Spinner 2 R _____   B _____   G _____

Spinner 3 R _____   B _____   G _____

2. (a) Now make the spinners from card and colour them as you did in question 1. Spin each spinner 20 times. Use tallying to record the number of times you get each colour.

Spinner	Red	Blue	Green
1			
2			
3			

(b) How closely do your results match the theoretical probabilities from question 1? Describe any differences. _____

_____

(c) Add your results to those of your partner. Do the results match the theoretical probabilities more closely? _____

NOW TRY THIS!

- You can use a computer program or calculator to generate random single-digit numbers. Write the theoretical probability of getting each number.
- ▦ Generate 10 numbers. Compare your results with the theoretical probabilities.
- ▦ Generate 50 and then 100 numbers. Compare again. What do you notice?

 You can work out the **theoretical probability** if there are **equally likely outcomes** (for example, if a spinner is just as likely to fall on one side as any other). To work out the theoretical probability of getting a particular colour, find the proportion of the spinner which is that colour.

Answers

p 8

A1 Suggested answers:
   (a) conduct a survey
   (b) find data
   (c) do an experiment
   (d) find data
   (e) do an experiment
   (f) conduct a survey
   (g) conduct a survey
   (h) conduct a survey
   (i) find data
   (j) conduct a survey/do an experiment
   (k) conduct a survey

p 16

A1 (a) 4
   (b) 1, 1, 2, 2, 3, 3, 3, 4, 4, 4, 4, 5
   (c) 3
   (d) 4

A2 (a) Mode = 2
     Median = 2   Range = 4
   (b) Mode = 1
     Median = 2   Range = 3
   (c) Mode = 4
     Median = 4   Range = 3
   (d) Modal values = 2 and 4
     Median = 3   Range = 7
   (e) Modal values = 0 and 3
     Median = 2.5 Range = 7

B (a) Mode
   (b) 5

p 17

C (c) 6, 6
   (f) 4, 4
   (i) 6, 6
   (m) 6, any digit between 6 and 9
   (n) 6
   The other questions have various possible answers.

Now try this!
2, 7
3, 5

p 18

A1 4

A2 (a) 5
   (b) 2
   (c) 4
   (d) 3 and 4

B1 (a) 6th   (b) 8th
   (c) 14th   (d) 17th
   (e) 21st   (f) 18th

B2 All are possible strategies.

p 19

C1 (a) 35
   (b) 18th
   (c) 4

C2 Village A   11
                 6th
                 2
     Village B   13
                 7th
                 5
     Village C   39
                 20th
                 4
     Village D   33
                 17th
                 2
     Village E   37
                 19th
                 4
     Village F   49
                 25th
                 3

Now try this!
Village A   Range is 3, mode is 1
Village B   Range is unknown, modal values are 4, 5, 6
Village C   Range is 6, mode is 5
Village D   Range is 4, mode is 2
Village E   Range is unknown, mode is 4
Village F   Range is 5, mode is 2

p 20

A (a) 25   (b) 28   (c) 29
   (d) 28   (e) 29   (f) 27.5
   (g) 30.9   (h) 27.625   (i) 29.4375

B (a) 2.4   (b) 3.7
   (c) 3.3   (d) 5.1
   (e) 5.3   (f) 5

p 21

C1 (a) 2   (b) 9   (c) 8   (d) 1

C2 (a) 49
   (b)

25	26	27	28	29	30	31	32	33	34+
0	2	5	9	10	12	8	2	1	0
0	52	135	252	290	360	248	64	33	0

   (c) 1434
   (d) 29.3

C3 (a) Callous High

25	26	27	28	29	30	31	32	33+	Total
0	1	1	6	9	11	10	11	0	49
0	26	27	168	261	330	310	352	0	1474

Mean = **30.1**

   (b) Low Lea Road

25	26	27	28	29	30	31	32	33+	Total
0	2	1	4	8	10	9	14	0	48
0	52	27	112	232	300	279	448	0	1450

Mean = **30.2**

(c) Miserly Park

25	26	27	28	29	30	31	32	33+	Total
2	1	4	3	7	15	11	12	0	55
50	26	108	84	203	450	341	384	0	1646

Mean = **29.9**

Now try this!
(a) Any two numbers with a total of 5
(b) Any two numbers with a total of 17

p 22

A1 **(b)** Frequency
3
6
20
8
12
1
(c) 14
(d) 47
(e) 8

A2 **(a)** 12%   **(b)** 16%

A3 **(a)** $\frac{2}{5}$ **(b)** $\frac{3}{50}$

p 23

C1 **(a)** There would only be one or two in each category.
(b)

Number of pounds	Frequency
£10–£14	3
£15–£19	5
£20–£24	6
£25–£29	4
£30–£34	2

(c) £20–£24
(d) 6
(e) Yes
$\frac{3}{10}$
Yes
$\frac{1}{10}$

p 24

A1 **(a)** 3   **(b)** 5

A2 2

p 25

C1 **(a)** Frequency
8
16
4
16
6
(b) e and o
(c) 12

C2 **(a)** Frequency
11
13
6
12
8
(b) e

p 26

A1 **(a)** 48   **(b)** 299
(c) 49   **(d)** 312

A2 **(a)** 7 May   **(b)** 31 May
(c) 17 May   **(d)** 19 May

A3 20 May and 9 May

A4 24 May

A5 It was a bank holiday.

B1 Frequency
16
0
4
8
3

p 27

C1 **(a)** 802   **(b)** 812
(c) 681   **(d)** 863
(e) 3425

C2 28 June

C3 1 June and 26 June

C4 8 June and 16 June

C5 **(a)** 59.8   **(b)** 55.5
(c) 271.5   **(d)** 222.6

C6 114.2

p 28

A1 **(a)** $\frac{1}{8}$ **(b)** Vegetables
(c) $\frac{1}{5}$ **(d)** Fruit and 'Other'

A2 $\frac{1}{2}$

B1 **(a)** Not known (not enough information given)
(b) True
(c) Not known (not enough information given)
(d) True

B2 **(a)** True   **(b)** True

p 29

C1 **(a)** $\frac{1}{4}$
(b) Birds' eggs
(c) Small animals

C2 **(a)** $\frac{1}{8}$
(b) Fruit
(c) $\frac{1}{2}$

C3 **(a)**

Day 3	Kilograms
Fruit	1.475
Birds' eggs	0.025
Small animals	0.4
Insects	0.025
Plant matter	1.675

(b) The pie chart would look the same.

p 30

All answers are approximate.

A1 (a) 40   (b) 95   (c) 130   (d) 200

A2 30

A3 130

A4 760

A5 (a) 500
(b) 260
(c) £3920

B1 (a) 543   (b) 464   (c) £5074.50

p 31

C1 (a) Friday, Saturday, Sunday
(b) Because it's the weekend

C2 Approximate answers:
(a) £17 300   (b) £27 600

C3 Just over $\frac{3}{5}$ or nearly $\frac{2}{3}$

C4 (b) Tuesday, Thursday

Now try this!
Approximate answers:
£60 620
12 124

p 32

A1 Approximate answers:
(a) 6250   (b) 2100   (c) 5000   (d) 8000

A2 (a) 1995   (b) 1990, 1998, 2002
(c) 1991, 1999   (d) 2001

B1 (a) 1992–1994

B2 (a) They increased gradually year on year.
(b) They decreased sharply.

B3 They rise slowly and fall quickly.

B4 Possible reasons include lack of food, increase in
number of predators, weather conditions, pollution.

p 33

C1 (a) 1997–1998   (b) 1994–1995
(c) 1991–1992   (d) 2001–2002

C2 Approximate answers:
(a) 2500   (b) 3400

p 34

A1 Total
79
71
124
86

A2 (a) U-phoric   (b) X-cite
(c) U-phoric   (d) U-phoric

A3 (a) 4th
(b) Probably because of Christmas

A4 (a) Possibly as a result of a special promotion or
advertising
(b) Two of them fell.

A5 Pie chart

B2 (a) 20%   (b) 30%

B3 (a) $\frac{1}{5}$ (b) $\frac{1}{4}$

p 35

C1 (a) Total
79
71
124
86
(b) 360 000

C2 (a) 79°

Now try this!

	2002	2003
D-lite	20	19.75
N-tice	23.25	17.75
U-phoric	27	31
X-cite	20.5	21.5

p 36

A1 Approximate answers:
(a) $\frac{1}{4}$ (b) $\frac{1}{3}$
(c) $\frac{1}{10}$ (d) $\frac{1}{3}$

A2 Hard to say without further information (such as
temperature) but it is unlikely to be summer.

A3 No

A4 Approximate answers:
(a) 7 or 8   (b) 10
(c) 3   (d) 10

B (a) Probably summer
(b) 30
(c) Yes, because the pie chart shows that approximately
one-third of the days had scattered cloud, and the
maximum this could be is 10 days. The bar chart
shows 12 days with scattered cloud.

p 37

C1 Approximate answers:
(a) $\frac{1}{3}$ (b) $\frac{1}{6}$ (c) $\frac{1}{16}$
(d) $\frac{1}{16}$ (e) $\frac{1}{4}$ (f) $\frac{1}{8}$

C2 Approximate answers:
(a) 40%   (b) 10%   (c) 4%
(d) 20%   (e) 10%   (f) 16% or 17%

C3 (a) Can't tell
(b) True
(c) True
(d) Can't tell
(e) False
(f) False

Now try this!
(a) FlyCheap   (b) About the same   (c) FlyFar
(d) FlyCheap   (e) FlyFar   (f) FlyCheap

p 38

A1 (a) Gym   (b) Yoga

A2 (a) 64%   (b) 45%   (c) 28%

A3 (a) 28%   (b) 23%   (c) 60%

A4 (a) 8%   (b) 32%   (c) 12%

B It would be best to choose the activities with the longest
white bars on the chart; these are the activities that
relatively few people currently do, but many would
consider doing.

p 39

C2 (a) 64%   (b) 39%
      (c) 45%   (d) 61%
      (e) 16%   (f) 38%
      (g) 32%   (h) 80%

p 40

All answers are approximate.

A1 (a) 8%   (b) 18%   (c) 27%   (d) 37%

A2 (a) $\frac{1}{10}$ (b) $\frac{1}{5}$ (c) $\frac{1}{4}$ (d) $\frac{1}{3}$ or $\frac{2}{5}$

A3 (a) 75%   (b) 93%   (c) 66%   (d) 84%

B1 (a) 200   (b) 110
      (c) 49   (d) 17
      (e) 33   (f) 253

B2 (a) 600   (b) 440
      (c) 441   (d) 34
      (e) 67   (f) 759

B3 Linz

p 41

C1 Approximate answers:
      (a) 96%   (b) 98%   (c) 97%   (d) 96%
      (e) 98%   (f) 94%   (g) 93%   (h) 90%

C2 Approximate answers:
      (a) 13   (b) 50
      (c) 12   (d) 28
      (e) 5   (f) 52
      (g) 17   (h) 1

C3 3898

C4 Approximately 178

C5 Approximate answers:
      (a) $\frac{1}{20}$
      (b) 5%

Now try this!

The survey collected data for more Linz cars than Schwaz cars. A larger sample gives more reliable results.

p 42

A (a) 1
    (b) 3
    (c) 2.9

B1

	Border Collie	Poodle
Mean	6.1	6.1
Range	4	6

p 43

C1 (a) 7   8   7
      (b) 8   10   5

C2 There is not enough information given to prove or disprove the statement.

p 44

A1 (a) 7   15
      (b) 7   30   42   112   55   60   35   16   18   60
      (c) 435
      (d) 4.35

B1 Second row:
      2   15
      Last row:
      2   30   48   72   65   48   49   56   45   50   11   24   13
      (Total 513)
      Mean = 5.13

B2 Article A: range is 9
      Article B: range is 12

p 46

A Answers depend on current year.

p 50

A (a) ✓ 6   (b) ✓ 52
    (c) ✓ 2   (d) ×
    (e) ×   (f) ×
    (g) ✓ 2   (h) ×
    (i) ✓ 2   (j) ×

B1 (a) $\frac{1}{8}$ (b) $\frac{1}{8}$
     (c) $\frac{3}{8}$ (d) $\frac{1}{4}$ or $\frac{2}{8}$
     (e) 0   (f) $\frac{1}{8}$

B4 The following numbers in any order: 1, 1, 3, 5, 5, 5, 6, 6

p 51

C1 (a) 8
      (b) Yes
      (c) A $\frac{2}{8}$ or $\frac{1}{4}$ E $\frac{1}{8}$ L $\frac{3}{8}$ P $\frac{1}{8}$ R $\frac{1}{8}$

C2 (a) $\frac{1}{8}$ (b) $\frac{2}{8}$ or $\frac{1}{4}$
     (c) $\frac{3}{8}$ (d) $\frac{3}{8}$
     (e) $\frac{2}{8}$ or $\frac{1}{4}$ (f) $\frac{3}{8}$
     (g) $\frac{5}{8}$ (h) $\frac{6}{8}$ or $\frac{3}{4}$
     (i) $\frac{1}{8}$ (j) $\frac{4}{8}$ or $\frac{1}{2}$
     (k) $\frac{3}{8}$ (l) $\frac{1}{8}$

p 52

A1 (a) 2, $\frac{1}{2}$
      (b) 7, $\frac{2}{7}$
      (c) 6, $\frac{3}{6}$ or $\frac{1}{2}$
      (d) 12, $\frac{6}{12}$ or $\frac{1}{2}$
      (e) 4, $\frac{1}{4}$
      (f) 52, $\frac{13}{52}$ or $\frac{1}{4}$
      (g) 52, $\frac{4}{52}$ or $\frac{1}{13}$

C1 (a) $\frac{1}{40}$ (b) $\frac{1}{8}$

     (c) $\frac{1}{10}$ (d) $\frac{1}{40}$

     (e) $\frac{2}{5}$ (f) $\frac{1}{5}$

     (g) $\frac{3}{40}$ (h) $\frac{1}{20}$

     (i) $\frac{9}{20}$ (j) $\frac{1}{10}$

     (k) $\frac{7}{40}$ (l) $\frac{1}{2}$

     (m) $\frac{3}{4}$ (n) $\frac{1}{2}$

C2 (a) The same
     (b) The same

C3 (a) $\frac{1}{16}$ (b) $\frac{5}{16}$

     (c) $\frac{1}{4}$ (d) $\frac{1}{16}$

     (e) $\frac{3}{16}$ (f) $\frac{1}{8}$

A1 2, 3, 4, 5, 6, 7, 8, 9, 10, 11, 12

A2 (a) 12
     (b) 2

Now try this!

A total of 7 is most likely.

(a) $\frac{1}{6}$ (b) $\frac{1}{36}$

(c) $\frac{1}{12}$ (d) $\frac{5}{36}$

A1 (a) $\frac{1}{4}$ (b) $\frac{1}{2}$ (c) $\frac{1}{4}$

A2 (a) 2 or 3   (b) 12 or 13   (c) 25

A3 (a) 5   (b) 25   (c) 50

A1 101   102   103   103   104   104   105   105   106   107

A2

Total	101	102	103	104	105	106	107
Probability	$\frac{1}{10}$	$\frac{1}{10}$	$\frac{1}{5}$	$\frac{1}{5}$	$\frac{1}{5}$	$\frac{1}{10}$	$\frac{1}{10}$

B1 (a) 15

B2 (a) $\frac{1}{15}$

     (b) $\frac{2}{15}$

     (c) $\frac{1}{5}$

B3 (a) $\frac{1}{5}$

     (b) $\frac{2}{5}$

     (c) $\frac{2}{5}$